# BALANCING FAMILY SCREEN TIME

THE COMPLETE INTERACTIVE COLLECTION — TIPS AND TRICKS TO INSTILL A HEALTHY RELATIONSHIP WITH DEVICES

ELIZABETH ERNST DENSLEY, BSN

EBook ISBN: 978-1-7342589-8-1

Trade Paperback ISBN: 978-1-7342589-5-0

Published by Sixpack LLC

Sixpack LLC EBook Edition 2022

Sixpack LLC Trade Paperback Edition 2022

Printed in the USA

# CONTENTS

*This book is dedicated to my grandchildren who taught me that there is something worse than the loud chaos of a family gathering together—SILENCE. As every parent or mentor learns, silence is often an indicator of "trouble," and we need to check on our beautiful children pronto. Our house was filled with thirty-three family members, and yet it was quiet. They were all lost in their devices—a virtual world filled with information of all kinds, threats, and addiction. It is time to balance the virtual world with reality so we don't find ourselves lost in it.*

# INTRODUCTION

Zombies are real! Just ask my seventeen-year-old grandson. He can describe how a germ, chemical, gas, or radiation changes people and how zombies are now walking the earth. I have to wonder why or how he created such a crazy belief system, and yet, he seems unafraid. On the other hand, I have proof that zombies do exist. They visit my home regularly.

I am a grandmother of nineteen grandchildren ranging in age from the early twenties and married down to an adorable two-year-old girl with a round face and unending curiosity. You can imagine the noise when this many children gather in one place and get so excited to spend time together. The screams of delight, giggles, and serious conversations about the latest and greatest things echo off our vaulted ceiling. It's crazy, but I love it. Until one day, it all stopped.

As I finished preparing for one of our family meals, I paused. Something wasn't right. I placed my knife on the counter and walked through the house. There, in various nooks and crannies, sat a child or a small group of children completely lost in the devices they now held in their hands. My stomach turned, and my heart broke at the thought of what this meant for my grandchildren's future. Even some of the parents were busily scrolling through their devices, silent and detached.

This wasn't the first time my Spidey senses had tingled and a red flag of warning waved frantically in my head, but this time, as the grandmother, an entire generation stood between the perceived enemy and me. The most I could do at this point was to verify whether this fear was valid. So I waited and watched. It was just a game, right?

I watched as my then thirteen-year-old grandson hid in his room, alone, just him and his video games, day after day.

This same boy at fourteen finally went out to play touch football with the scouts. I was so excited to see him get out and interact with the other boys. I offered to take care of his phone so it didn't get broken or lost in the excitement of the game. I wasn't prepared for what came next—his reaction. You would have thought I asked him to cut off his arm. The instant anger and verbal attack were harsh and completely uncharacteristic of him. That red flag was waving so fast it made a sonic boom go off in my head. At least I didn't have to worry about the phone. After that response, there wasn't a safer place for it than in that boy's care.

One night, my now seventeen-year-old grandson finally came out of his room. I was excited until I looked at his face; gray pallor and dark circles under his sunken eyes. The air from his room was stale and warm. No fresh air or sunshine. Practically no activity and minimal interaction with real people and reality. Even he couldn't deny how bad he looked.

I would often walk into the family room and see the kids lounging on the couch playing on the phone with the iPad in their laps and the TV on. To take away even one of those devices triggered them. I used to think multitasking was an excellent efficiency skill, but not in this case; instead, it creates a solid inability to focus on one thing at a time, like school-work or reading.

I've refereed innumerable wars over which grandchild's turn it was on the various devices. In fact, it became a regular part of sibling interaction: arguing over whose turn it was to pick the show on TV, which game to play, or heaven forbid, when someone messed up someone else's game. I hated the lying and manipulation that went on while the children attempted to get their way.

There would be times I would call for a fifteen-minute timeout to reset a situation that had gotten out of control. This would escalate the tantrums, and I became the target of their anger. When I think they can't get any more out of control, they prove me wrong; screaming and throwing things, complaining about how unfair it is, how they hate me because I'm so mean and unreasonable. But I have learned to hold my ground, and the devices stay off.

The next thing that happens in the above scenario is that my grandson can't handle having his device out of his hands. I put the tablet on the kitchen table, less than twenty feet away and in clear sight. You can't ignore that there is something wrong when a child has lost complete control. I can see his little mind strategizing how best to get his device back and it wasn't by cooperating.

Needless to say, I stopped watching and began to research and learn. I tried various ways to decrease screen time and get the kids up and doing something —anything. It is an ongoing battle, but one worth fighting for. My fear for their physical and mental health made me want to take all their devices away. I became jaded, and the introduction of social media and its effects, not just on teens, wasn't helping that opinion.

Our teens are becoming more and more emotionally fragile, making them incapable of coping with even the simplest of life's bumps. In his book, *Disconnected: How to Protect Your Kids from the Harmful Effects of Device Dependency,*[1] Thomas Kersting, a high school counselor, reported that a young girl came to him, totally distraught because someone had called her a name. Counseling and medications for anxiety and depression are now common in our schools. Teen suicides have increased dramatically. No wonder technology is being blamed for all this chaos. However, though technology may play a significant role in our children's ability to process emotions, to completely ban our children's technology use is not only unrealistic, but not going to solve every aspect of the problem. We also need to address the other factors in this equation that are affecting our children's lack of emotional control. But what I have learned is that it's never just one thing and that we need to find the other factors in this equation and address them as well.

Technology is not going to go away. If anything, it will progress at an even faster rate. It is a part of our world, especially the world of our children. They know nothing else. So, I adjusted my focus to becoming more aware and taking on the responsibility of creating balance. I realized that when fear determines how I react, I am more likely to respond rashly rather than act in my child's best interest. Instead of fighting and being afraid for our children, I've embraced the idea that technology is a tool within our lives. All tools have user manuals and warnings. When we use them correctly, they become an effective part of our lives, uplifting and assisting us as we strive to grow through challenges; we find the strength to allow our children to build positive and happy futures for themselves and their families. Dr. Jean Twenge says that technology "should be a tool you use, not a tool that uses you."[2]

I'm a nursery nurse, and one of the first things I teach my new moms is this: you will hear many ways to deal with the same "problem." None of them are wrong. People are simply sharing their experiences and what they believe to be true and helpful. Instead of getting frustrated, place all of these different ideas into a gunny sack, shake it all up, and try them out one at a time until you find the one that works best for you and your family. That is true for everything, including screen time.

In this book, I will share what I've learned from experts in this field as well as parents who have worked their way through this situation. Be patient, and don't expect a magical result without any effort on your part. This is a huge undertaking. Rome wasn't built in a day. Unlearning something, especially a habit, is a significant challenge. You only have a limited amount of time to help your child become a strong, responsible, effective, caring, and loving adult. Focus on your desired result: a child that grows up strong in body and mind and able to adapt as life changes. Envision him/her standing strong against adversity and finding true joy, living a balanced life, and sharing that with the next generation.

If you are a parent, grandparent, teacher, mentor, or guardian, this book is for you. However, your perceived expectations of what's inside these pages may tarnish its appeal. When searching for a solution to a problem, I find that I often have an invisible expectation of what I will find acceptable. I place myself in a box, rejecting the very information I was looking for. I don't want to think about the thousands of dollars I've spent doing this, then being disappointed that I've made no headway whatsoever.

Please, don't just read this book—experience it. As you go through each section or chapter, stop and make the discoveries you need to get the answers you are looking for. Keep your eyes on the prize and how much you want it.

This book becomes interactive, starting with chapter 3. The workbook is where the magic happens. As you interact and do the work required to create change, you will begin to move toward your goal of balancing screen time in your home (or any other goal or challenge you may face) by applying the principles and action steps. You, together with the ones you care about most, will make amazing discoveries that can make your dreams come true if you fight for them. Pace yourselves accordingly; each family reacts in their own way. Achieving one small step at a time is all it takes to keep moving forward. It is the key to your success.

WARNING! Your subconscious is going to put up a fight. It wants you to be comfortable and safe, and you will be challenging the familiar. Everything we do here is meant to convince your mind that these are the changes you want to make to achieve your goal. Your subconscious will challenge that, so get ready to fight back and give it the necessary information to allow these changes. Old programs and beliefs will haunt you, like "journaling is boring," "these assignments are stupid," "I'll just think about it in passing." Don't let your body or bio-computer defeat your soul's higher desires to grow and soar.

Note: The header for all the chapters starting in chapter 3 is the Confidence Heart. It is there to remind you about the progress you're making and the tools you have available to help you achieve your goal. You have undertaken a great challenge and I salute you for that.

# 1 STEVE JOBS AND BILL GATES RAISE THEIR CHILDREN TECH-FREE

When I first heard that Steve Jobs and Bill Gates were raising their children tech-free, I assumed these brilliant men who put all the intricate pieces together that make up most of the technology we use today knew the side effects, especially on our children. And yet, they continued to create games and apps that drew us in, all in the name of money. It wouldn't be the first time a company, like our sub-conscious, provided us with what we wanted, whether it was good for us or not. It made me angry.

On the other hand, I could see them as people who could make my dreams come true. When I was a child, going to the drive-in was the best treat ever. I would go dressed in my pjs, Mom would have packed up dinner and treats, and we would get there early enough to get a good spot and play on the playground. Sometimes, they even had rides like a carousel. When it finally got dark enough, Daddy would hang the speaker on the car window, and we waited. Suddenly, the screen would come alive, and like magic, a story would unfold. Tired, but disappointed it was over, we would drive home, and I would wish I could watch the movie again. Men like Steve Jobs and Bill Gates made that dream come true.

As a teenager, I would meet my girlfriends every Saturday, each time at someone else's house somewhere in the Salt Lake Valley. Oh, how I wished I had a phone or some way of getting help while I was aimlessly circling the neighborhood for the address. Again, in response to a need, technology provided us with a way not only to communicate with others, but our phones verbally talk us through the directions we asked for. Another dream come true.

We are never satisfied. We can always take what we have and add the sentence: "I wish it could . . ." When Netflix came out, we were limited to watching what they offered and waited for them to arrive in the mailbox. Wouldn't it be cool if, somehow, we could watch almost any movie, at any time, in any place? Voila, streaming apps became readily available.

During the COVID-19 pandemic, technology became a lifesaver for many businesses and schools. It kept us connected. A blessing for sure, but with every invention ever created, a negative side is always evident. So, rather than blaming the progress technology affords us, let us look at ourselves and how we manage that gift. Just because alcohol, drugs, and cigarettes are available doesn't mean we should use them without thought or purpose.

Yes, Steve Jobs, Bill Gates, and many others have refused to let their children use their incredible inventions. Some expressed concern only after their child got obsessed with a game and started showing personality and behavioral changes. Steve Jobs only allowed his children to use desktop computers and generally only for school. Handheld devices were never allowed. Because of this belief, he sent his children to Montessori schools and spent many hours reading and educating his children about the world around them.

An article in *Business Insider* reads, "In a recent interview on the online news channel Cheddar, iPod co-creator Tony Fadell speculated that if Steve Jobs were alive today, he'd want to address growing societal concerns about tech addiction. He'd say, 'Hey, we need to do something about it,' Fadell said." [1] On YouTube, there is a TedTalk video that discusses the same topic if you are interested. [2]

I believe Steve understood or would have quickly discovered why his devices had such adverse effects, especially on children. [3] He would also know the deeper causes and that he couldn't fix it by inventing more technology or taking a magic, anti-screen-effects pill. I believe Steve would use his technology to educate and encourage people to decide for themselves, much like the warning on a pack of cigarettes.

# 2 THE BRAIN AND HOW IT WORKS

You may have heard the phrase "informed consent." In the medical world, doctors and nurses strive to make sure patients understand their situations, options, and the possible consequences of the medication, diet, or procedure a doctor is suggesting so they can make an informed decision before moving on. In researching screen time, I have discovered the possible physical and emotional effects it can have on children. So now, we need to have a brief physiology and child development lesson so you can better determine what you think about the information and how that affects what you will do next. Don't worry, I'll keep it simple.

Primitive Reflexes

Let's start from the very beginning. Many of you may have had the opportunity to watch as the nurse or doctor checked out your beautiful new baby literally from head to toe. We check to see if they have all ten toes and fingers and if everything is in proper condition. We also check their primitive reflexes. Reflexes are essential to maintain life, and they're the foundation of what comes next. They include the ability to suck, grasp, and startle.

As a child gains control and uses his or her muscles, that movement is linked directly to his or her developmental growth. For example, we ask our new parents never to put their babies on their stomachs in hopes of preventing sudden infant death syndrome. Over time, studies have found that children who spent very little time on their abdomen were developmentally delayed by a year. When a child isn't allowed on his or her abdomen, they can't develop their neck and arm muscles or learn to balance and twist. Once allowed to lie on their stomachs, these babies quickly caught up.

It has also been discovered that a baby can only learn a language if he or she has physical interaction with the teacher/caregiver.[1] Watching the exact same exchange on a screen is completely ineffective. We are social animals requiring positive touch and eye contact. A child mirrors their environment.

Every experience, whether physical or emotional, is recorded in your child's brain, and your child becomes the person you showed them to become. They may not be able to speak or process this incoming information; however, they are being programmed.

This same process continues through adulthood. Whenever a physical motion connects to a thought or emotion, the mind sets that memory or ability much more quickly. Mentors often ask you to journal, combining your thoughts with physical action. It alerts the mind that this information is essential and needs to be uploaded to our programming. Without the physical piece, it is simply a fleeting thought that passes by.

## Body Versus Soul

Human beings are complex creatures. If we were to act and react according to our programming only, we would be robotic, unable to create our life's path. We would lack the "why" for what we want or where we want to go. Our souls make each of us unique and able to reach any goal we aspire to. It is our old programming that holds us back. Think about a pair of identical twins. Physically, they are precisely the same. Their experiences are similar, but how they process that experience is often very different. They have very different personalities, likes, and dislikes. It is their soul that makes them unique.

Have you ever sat on your couch watching TV and the thought crosses your mind that you should get up and do something? A battle takes place inside you between your programming and your soul. Your body or subconscious wants to be happy and comfortable, while your soul wants to stretch and grow. It wants you to reach your full potential, which only happens by getting out of your comfort zone. So do you get up, or do you stay and watch whatever comes next on your sixty-five-inch screen?

We collect experiences through our physical body —our senses—which are then stored and interpreted in our brain. Let me share an analogy with you. Imagine you go to a restaurant and order your favorite super spicy fajita, which you enjoy through your physical body: smell, sight, touch, taste, maybe even hearing as your fajita sizzles in the hot pan. You go home only to discover that your stomach didn't appreciate the abuse and revolts with severe indigestion and heartburn. Your mind takes note and stores this adverse reaction for future reference.

A week later, you find yourself at the same restaurant. You remember your previous experience, determined not to make the same mistake. Your friends are all bragging about getting the fiery fajita with extra jalapeños. The battle begins. Your programming reminds you of your previous discomfort. It also reminds you that saving face among your friends is a must. Your subconscious calculates all the pros and cons of this decision. In the end, you will most likely pick the choice that will make you the happiest at that moment, no matter the consequences. What's that all about? "Why am I so stupid? I knew better," escapes your lips as you once again find yourself completely miserable, waiting for your antacid to take effect, just as before.

What do you think your soul's input would have been? The one that you never even considered in this circumstance. Yup, it would have taken the higher ground, the path that causes you to grow: the self-control to choose what's best for you over what's most immediate or comfortable. Don't be so hard on yourself. We all do it.

People like to say it's not your fault, but it is in your control if you know what's going on in your head. You have been writing programs since before you were born. Did you know that you can learn to delete and rewrite old programs so they will better serve you?

You can't change what you don't understand.

Let's say your car makes a weird noise and runs roughly, so you get under the hood and look around, clang on the engine with your screwdriver, get frustrated, slam the hood down, and turn the key. Driving down the street, you discover that your assessment and mechanical skill haven't made a bit of difference. This book isn't about reducing your screen addiction as much as it is about how you can become the person with the knowledge and skills to help yourself achieve that goal. It is a manual with options and explanations that are the tools you need to fix your car, so to speak. If you don't know what the alternator does or how it works or maybe even that it exists, you can't address the problem. This manual informs you how you operate, how to become more aware, and how best to approach your screen time concerns.

If the voices in our heads argue back and forth about the simple act of getting off the couch, can you imagine the tug of war that will go on inside your head when you present it with the idea of decreasing screen time?

Your soul will be jumping for joy: "Hooray! We can finally move forward and become our best selves." Your body will set the brakes and refuse to do anything different or make you uncomfortable. Are you ready to battle for control, or are you going to let old programming drag you down to complacency?

## Subconscious Versus Conscious

Your bio-computer is the intricate machine where the battle of body versus soul takes place. Draw a circle on a piece of paper then divide it horizontally across the middle. The top half represents the conscious part of your brain, which processes approximately forty thousand bits per second, in comparison to your subconscious, which computes over four million bits per second. Its primary directive is, "Keep Linda happy, comfortable, and safe at all times!" There's one drawback; the subconscious focuses on the now and cannot or does not judge right from wrong. So that trip to the Mexican restaurant results in eating the super spicy fajita so you can look tough like the other guys. Later on, you consciously justify your choice as worth it because you enjoyed the food while looking good in front of your friends, reinforcing your choice as a good one, even though you paid for it with indigestion. Like Spock from *Star Trek* always says, "It's not logical."

## Reward System: Dopamine

When *Tetris* and *Pacman* first came out, we played for fun—a game of skill. Even I could feel the draw of needing to best myself, playing again and again, shooting for that perfect score. I became more and more obsessed with it. Why? Today, we know the answer. Every time I scored, my brain released a tiny drop of dopamine as a reward. Little did I know that the need to feel rewarded is a program hardwired inside us, and this game was providing that, filling a basic human need. If Tetris stimulated just a tiny drop of dopamine, can you imagine what the games of today can do? Take a single shooter game, for instance. Imagine the amount of dopamine that the game elicits. We not only want, but need, more. And it works precisely like morphine or any street drug: our bodies adapt to the current dose and then require more to get the same response, the same high. So gaming companies create games that fill that need—more graphic, more intense, more deadly, more exciting to create a reaction that releases the amount of dopamine the player now requires to keep him or her engaged.

Another basic need is that of acceptance. Each time our phone beeps, it reinforces the feeling that we are seen and accepted. Dopamine is released to verify that that need is being fulfilled. So we text or tweet more often, hoping to get more responses. As we consider pulling back from gaming and screen time, the first challenge is changing the familiar, or our habits, and the second is going through a literal withdrawal from dopamine.

Let's add one more twist to all of this. Remember how I told you that the subconscious doesn't judge right from wrong, it just records everything as fact? It has one purpose, and that is to keep you safe, happy, and comfortable, and your subconscious will manipulate you into getting your own way. Saying "It's just a game" or "I only shoot bad guys" makes shooting someone acceptable and becomes a justification protecting your belief system that murder and mayhem are wrong. Texting and tweeting my friends is a good thing, except it's keeping me from interacting with the people around me. Our subconscious craves excitement and novelty which our devices provide.

The RAS, the reticular activating system, which is the filter that protects the subconscious from overload, is not impenetrable. If a message is repeated often enough, it will eventually be allowed through and filed away as fact. "Zombies are real." Once these ideas are accepted as facts, you will act on them. So as my grandchildren play for hours on their devices, I have to ask what they are being taught. How are their young minds being programmed? Does it fit within their family's value system? It's not just the time spent, but how the time is spent.

Neuroplasticity

The good news is that despite all that we've discussed, we can rewrite old programs that no longer serve us because of neuroplasticity.[2]

Your brain is adaptable. Even though you may have pathways or beliefs that are very established, like, "spinach is gross," you can change those beliefs. You decide it's time to eat healthier and spinach is an excellent vegetable to add to your diet. At first, you're hesitant and sneak a little into your shake. Mm-mmm, that's not so bad, so you add a little more, turning your shake a strange color, but it tastes good. Soon, you add spinach to soups and casseroles, and eventually, you enjoy baby spinach salads. Each time you added spinach to your diet, it reinforced your new neural pathway, making it stronger, while shrinking the old path, "spinach is gross." This is why they say it takes at least twenty-eight days for a new idea to become a habit.

Each time you succeed, the body releases dopamine as a positive reinforcement, making you feel happy, accomplished, and strong, which encourages you to repeat that action again and reinforces your new neural pathway.

The same thing happens each time your phone beeps. It is a sign that you are being acknowledged and accepted—a basic human need. Even now, you can probably feel the conflict as you consider needing to rewrite these pathways. How to do that is a book in itself. Don't worry, it's all doable with a bit of determination, guidance, and a lot of patience, especially with yourself.

# 3 KNOWING WHAT MAKES YOUR CHILD TICK: HARDWIRED TO BE YOU

E very time I go to a seminar/webinar or read a book, I feel excited because, finally, I will get the answers I've been looking for, a checklist of to-dos, or even some don'ts. They present excellent information, like how to share a five-day challenge and build a coaching business, or how to overcome or prevent the mistakes that keep you from reaching a goal. Despite that, after the webinar, convention, or book, I always have to choose to actually put their teaching into action or nothing will change. I've learned that the magic isn't in their information; it's in me and my willingness to act on what I've learned.

For those who would prefer a simple checklist with concise and straightforward explanations, I apologize. You can't check off a list when it involves other people. You have complete control only over yourself. You can't control the baby that's experimenting every time he drops something from his highchair or protect the toddler from falling while she's learning to walk. You shouldn't protect your child from the penalties of not turning in their homework because they won't experience the consequences, keeping them from growing and adapting or becoming strong enough to endure adversity and change. What you can do is discover who your child is, how they tick, and what their emotional needs are. Use this information to help direct them to find the answers for themselves.

## Personality Styles

I can hear you yelling, "Oh my gosh, are you kidding me? Just tell me how to deal with screen time!" Maybe you are the "Just do it!" type. Strong and dominant, you focus on getting things done. We need strong leaders like you. Or maybe you are someone who needs to investigate thoroughly before acting. And perhaps you are a parent whose heart is so tender that you can't bear to see your child suffer. Can you relate to any of these? It reminds me of the movie *Divergent* or the different houses at Hogwarts, where they distinctly divide their communities by personality styles. Knowing your and your child's personality styles will help you find the right way to approach them. Understanding how you would work best together is even more effective. Let me share a short analogy.

I had to learn how to French braid my hair. I needed my mind and my fingers to coordinate and learn a new skill. I could see the steps in my mind. Imagine now that each finger is one of your children, your wife or husband, or your expectations. It starts out simple enough, comb out your hair. Next, separate your hair into three even sections. Your mind remembers and maybe even visualizes each step. Each finger moves you toward your goal, in this case, a beautiful braid.

Now, take the strand from the right side and place it over the middle one. You feel encouraged. This is a familiar move if you have ever experienced braiding something before. All fingers remain on board and follow your instructions. The next step is to bring the left strand over the middle one. "I've got this!" you think.

While holding and controlling all three strands with your non-dominant hand, grab a small section of hair just below the hair that you already pulled up on the right with the next section of hair about one inch wide. Add it to the strand you're holding on to the right. Do the same on the left side and repeat. Even if the strands remain in some manner of control, you probably will lose control of some of the separated strands of hair. All your fingers do their best, but they can't keep all the strands in order. Your fingers (children, spouse, yourself) cannot adapt, learn, and adjust to the new information, no matter how well they understand the how. Your hair begins to separate and your frustration rises until everyone finally screams, "Stop!"

Your pointer finger stands erect, frustrated that the others can't get their act together and cooperate. Your middle finger is desperately trying to list the steps it needs to perform. Your ring finger debates whether it is worth putting everyone else through the pain. Lastly, your pinkie giggles and finds the whole process hilarious and wants to try again. Can you see the different personality types? I bet you didn't consider that personality types would be a part of decreasing screen-time.

This change is not just about you and how you think things should proceed. It is also about your children, spouse, or even grandparents or friends. It's about how they react and understand the situation. Each one of them sees and understands it in their own way. Our base programming, which includes our personality styles, is hardwired. Understanding and addressing someone in their language will increase communication and cooperation a thousand times over.

You may realize that the just-do-it type clashes

with the sensitive, caring, soft-hearted style. The child who needs a specific list of the how and why will disagree with the fun-loving, let's-try-it-again type. We need to learn how to approach our children to elicit greater cooperation and decrease frustration. Knowing your child's personality type will help develop a plan of action that will move you toward your goal faster and with less resistance and frustration for all of you.

Have you ever had a teacher that could teach you something unique while making you laugh so hard it hurt? Dr. Robert Rohm is that teacher for me.[1] He developed the DISC method of personality styles. (D)ominance, (i)nfluence, (S)teadiness and (C)onscientiousness.[2] The following is how he helps you discover your personality style. I experienced this at a live presentation with Dr. Robert Rohm. He always clarifies that as you answer these questions, you may feel like you can be either and that your choice today is not set in stone, but a guideline to help you discover something about yourself.

- Draw a circle and divide it in half vertically. Dr. Rohm's first question is, "Do you believe you are more task-oriented or people-oriented?"
- If you are task-oriented, place yourself on

the left side of the circle; people-oriented on the right.
- Now, draw a line horizontally across your circle. Dr. Rohm's next question is, "Do you feel you are more of an extrovert or an introvert?
- Extroverts fall into the top half of the circle and introverts on the bottom.
- Use your responses to these two questions to mark which quadrant you best fit into.

If you find yourself in the left upper quadrant, you may be a "D" personality type: task-oriented, extroverted, dominant, directive, and driven. "D" types' motto is "Just get it done," and they do. A "D" or dominant type is a shaker and a mover. We need strong leaders that make us stretch and grow. Completing their task is what fills their tank.

Like everything else in this world, there is a flip side to every personality. The dominant type often comes across as rude, bossy, and cold-hearted. The only thing that seems to matter is the task, the bottom line. Finding a balance and awareness of the personalities of the people around "D" types will challenge their patience. Still, if controlled, they'll find their goals will be achieved faster and more efficiently, and co-workers will admire their leadership skills and ability to get things done.

If you're an extrovert but people-oriented, you will find yourself in the right upper quadrant, an "I" or inspiring type. People are naturally drawn to "I" types because their environment is fun, friendly, and accepting. They love being around people, talking, and being the center of attention; as they do this, they inspire others with their optimism.

As a society, we need these light-hearted and cheerful people to balance out the seriousness of life. Enjoying whatever they are doing and being surrounded by people makes them feel complete. However, to gain approval from others, the "I" type can become manipulative, unfocused, and excitable. When they find balance, this type can push our society forward. Optimism, imagination, and their ability to communicate can turn a negative situation into a community-building experience.

If you've met the kindest person in the world, he or she is probably an "S" or supportive type. They are people-oriented and introverted, living in the bottom right-hand quadrant. You feel safe and supported because they remain consistent, caring, and you can count on them to follow through. What is in your best interest is forever on their minds. Service is what fills them up.

Like the other personalities, the "S" type has a dark side. They can be easily manipulated and used by others due to their trusting nature. Discovering that they are being used or unappreciated brings out a monster that would put the "D" to shame. They find their inner voice in defense of another or the best interest of the group. When balanced, they are steadfast, reliable, systematic, and soft-hearted, putting humanity back into any equation.

Last, but definitely not least, are the amazing people who live within the bottom, left-hand quadrant: "C" or cautious types. They are the most innovative people you will ever meet. Without them, progress would be at a standstill, and that fantastic phone in your back pocket would not exist. They are introverted and focused on tasks. But what drives them the most is the need to be correct. Every decision includes extensive research. They are very detail-oriented and structured. As Dr. Rohm likes to point out, these are the people you want piloting a plane, performing surgery, or designing the family car. They often feel uncomfortable in crowds because they are seen as different and labeled as nerds, geeks, quirky, or weird when instead, they are brilliant. Be very appreciative of them.

In the end, we all need each other to share our talents and balance our society, and the truth is we are generally a blend of personality types. This blend makes you and your child unique in how you act and how you perceive and react to your surroundings. Understanding where your child, spouse, or friend is coming from allows you to approach them in their language. Have you ever had the thought, "He gets me!" That person was speaking to your personality type.

### Workbook 3A: Identify Personality Styles

First, discover who you are.

- What is your personality style?

_____

_____

_____

_____

_____

_____

- Describe a few of your strengths and weaknesses.

_____

_____

_____

_____

_____

_____

_____

_____

_____

- List which stage or stages you operate in:

_____

_____

_____

_____

_____

_____

Now, identify the personality styles of your family.

- What is the personality style of your significant other? Record it below:

_____

_____

_____

_____

_____

_____

- List which stage or stages your spouse
  operates in:

_____

_____

_____

_____

_____

_____

- How do your and your spouse's styles
  both clash and work well together? Is
  there a way to prevent future
  confrontation if you address this now?

_____

_____

_____

_____

_____

_____

_____

_____

- List each of your children's personality styles. How do your styles both clash and work well together? Is there a way to prevent future confrontation if you address this now?

Be sure to include assessments of others involved in these changes, such as grandparents, friends, teachers, or mentors.

Follow this example: The personality style of

_____ is _____ .

He/she most often operates in

_____ stage/stages.

_____

_____

_____

_____

_____

_____

_____

_____

_____

- Now answer for each child, how do your styles both clash and work well together? Is there a way to prevent future confrontation if you address this now?

_____

_____

_____

_____

_____

_____

_____

_____

_____

_____

_____

_____

## Love Language

There are five love languages; Words of Affirmation, Quality Time, Receiving Gifts, Acts of Service, and Physical Touch.

My ten-year-old grandson would always invite me to sit on the couch and watch cartoons with him. I've got things to do. I'm right here. I can see the TV from the kitchen. They are both rejections not of the invitation, but in his eyes, I have rejected him. Whatever I'm doing in the kitchen is more important than he is. I ignored his love language—the language of quality time.

Another example is when my sweet husband brings me flowers. They are nice, but in the depths of my soul, gifts feel conditional and don't speak my love language, words of affirmation. I always wanted to reject that idea because it felt selfish, but in the end, a nice compliment or a sign of appreciation is what makes me feel valued and loved. On the other hand, I show love through gifts and acts of service. We rarely give and receive in the same love language. It doesn't matter that it doesn't make sense; it only matters that we touch and connect with the people we love the most in a way that they can receive it fully. What is your child's love language?

· · ·

## Workbook 3B - Love Languages

Discover your love language and that of your family members. Go to https://www.5lovelanguages.com/learn.

- Use the lines below to record what you learn.

_____

_____

_____

_____

_____

_____

_____

_____

_____

_____

_____

_____

_____

## Stage Not Age

The last piece we need to consider before we approach our child is what stage of maturity or moral development they are in. It's about the stage rather than their actual age. Dr. Paul Jenkins, a positivity psychologist and life coach, shares this viewpoint. Rather than setting expectations by age alone, we need to discover what level of maturity or moral development our child is at. How many times have you said, "You're twelve years old; you should be able to do this by now." By creating an arbitrary expectation, we set ourselves and our child up for failure. Dr. Jenkins has divided the steps of maturity into three levels.[3]

**Stage 1: Self-centered**

This is not a derogatory word but rather a description. A baby learns that crying is the way to get what he or she needs to survive. As a toddler that belief is reinforced. They are focused on themselves, or are self-centered. This phase continues through all ages. Sometimes, I get so frustrated or tired that I just need things to go my way for a change. Can you relate to that? We are constantly flexing back and forth between stages, as do our children.

**Stage 2: Cooperation**

Your child has acquired the ability to respect others. They seek peace and can problem-solve a win-

win solution. When living in this stage, they can communicate, teach, and be taught; give them a little slack and positively acknowledge their abilities.

**Stage 3: Responsibility**

At this stage of moral development, we have the experience and ability to show empathy, give meaningful service, set moral principles, and do the right thing. We understand what we could not see before, including why our parents did what they did during our childhood, and now we are ready to ask for advice and their loving support.

**Workbook 3C: Stage Not Age—Maturity or Moral Development**

For the next few days, watch your children and yourself as you move through the various stages.

- Write down your observations.

_____

_____

_____

_____

_____

_____

_____

_____

_____

_____

_____

_____

_____

_____

_____

_____

_____

_____

_____

_____

_____

_____

_____

_____

_____

_____

_____

- If you can discover a reason you dropped a stage, write it down here. Being hungry or tired is often the reason we fall a level temporarily.

_____

_____

_____

_____

_____

_____

_____

_____

_____

_____

_____

_____

_____

_____

- Record your "a-ha" moments related to the "stage not age" concept:

_____

_____

_____

_____

_____

_____

_____

_____

_____

_____

_____

_____

_____

_____

_____

## Autism and Screen Time

Autism is a spectrum disorder, meaning it includes a range of linked conditions—everything from ADHD or "high functioning" to needing "substantial" or "very substantial support." Each child is unique as to strengths and weaknesses and has unique personalities and love languages. Their struggle with language skills and awkward social interaction are probably some of the more apparent signs. Considering how broad this group of unique human beings is, it isn't easy to give a straight answer that fits all responses. Like all children, they require:

- Consistency
- Repetition to learn and grow
- Time to adapt to the stimuli around them
- Space to recharge or regroup
- Predictable outcomes
- Ways to express themselves
- To be seen and accepted
- The feeling of control

The Autism Parenting Magazine included an article called "The Pros and Cons of Screen Time with ASD." It states that children with ASD spend 64.2% more time on screens than children not on the autism spectrum.[4] Here are a few points made in the article.

**Pros:**

- Digital devices provide an escape; here, they find predictable outcomes and perform at their own pace.
- Screens provide a buffer when using social media, allowing them to process the information in the real world.
- Video games offer repetition; they are predictable and often calming. Some may use it as a way to stimulate or regain emotional control.
- Screens can be used as a mode of therapy.
- It helps them learn without the distraction and anxiety of having so many others around them.

**Cons:**

- In children who are sensitive to stimuli, the noise, motion, and color of digital devices may irritate or worsen their behavior.
- Digital devices disrupt sleep patterns.
- Stress hormones are released when using screens, adding to their already inflamed nervous system.
- Children with ASD are more sensitive to

EMF, the electromagnetic frequency emitted by these devices.

- Devices hinder the skills needed for social interaction.
- Digital devices often lead to a delay in learning, and especially delayed speech since language programming only occurs when connected to human interaction.
- Screens exacerbate OCD and social anxiety.
- All the other effects of excessive screen time become apparent, including dopamine addiction.

I give you this as information only. Your situation is unique to you and is in your control. However, whenever possible, help your child come out into the world, getting fresh air, eating good food, and spending time playing together, practicing language, and social skills. Allow them to stretch to become the best they can be. You have been given this child as a blessing because you are the one who could best care for them.

## Our Youngest Screen Timers

No doubt you have heard of limiting screen time during the very tender and early years of a child's life. There are very few studies that can tell us how it will affect our young children. We know that screen time can delay speech. When we are spending time and interacting with them one-on-one, then and only then do they retain language. What else does it affect? Just because we don't know something doesn't mean it isn't happening.

Remember that a child's development connects to their physical activity. They need to play, touch, explore, and use all their senses to develop and learn. Allow them that. The occasional positive age-appropriate screen is part of their world. Find the right balance. For your information, I've listed the suggested time limitations given by www.childrens.com[5] and smartparentadvice.com:[6]

- 0-2 years: No screen time. Try to keep your child engaged in activities that will help them reach physical and developmental markers. (This may be unattainable if, since the day they were born, the mother holds both the baby and her phone lovingly in her arms. Children mirror their parents, so it's in your control how they see your screen time.)
- 2-5 years: Your child should be using screens for at most one hour of their day. Use this hour on high-quality educational

apps or children viewing programs. Try to keep your child engaged in activities that will help them reach physical and developmental markers.

- 6+ years: Limit screen time to two hours per day.

It is so much easier to establish family screen time rules when your children are young. Adjusting them as they get older gets complicated.

**UNIQUE TO YOU (Use these lines for extra notes or to strategize.)**

_____

_____

_____

_____

_____

_____

_____

_____

# 4  WHAT'S ALL THE FUSS ABOUT ANYWAY?

W hether you're a parent, grandparent, teacher, or mentor of any kind, you have probably noticed a change in our kids, and it's not a positive one; otherwise, you wouldn't even be reading this. Screen time has been questioned and studied since television came into play. By the 1960s, televisions were a part of almost every home. Generations have survived having a television in their homes. But mostly, no one thought to question this magical invention that was creating so much joy.

New technology came out so fast. After a while, we would see advertisements selling products only known by their initials, like the 2DS or MP3. It was assumed you knew what the heck they were. It was simple entertainment. So what is the fuss about? What is screen time, and why does it matter? Any device that has a screen falls into this category, including your television.

## Problem #1: It Draws Our Attention Away from Reality

Have you ever walked into a room and the sound of the TV caught your attention? You can't help but look to see what's going on. You are captivated with the need to know what comes next or which show it is. The next thing you know, you've been distracted for several minutes, if not sitting and entirely focused on it. Motion, lights, color, and intrigue capture our human sense of curiosity. We need to know what's new and what comes next.

I once heard someone say that her goal was to stop watching Hallmark movies. Not because they are bad, but because they drew her into a never-ending loop, playing shows 24/7 without any stops or breaks. We need something that indicates and signals our minds that it's time to stop and move on. Even television with all its commercials draws us into one big loop of shows.

## Problem #2: It Changes Our Programming

Humans pride themselves on being in control, having the freedom to choose. To be manipulated or to manipulate others is hurtful, and in some cases, harmful. Yet advertisers have been controlling what we believe since before radio and television. They are manipulating the options we have at any given time. If you are familiar with any of the home remodeling shows, you will hear comments and criticism about the design choices of previous eras. The wood paneling and orange and green themes of the seventies, the preference of hardwood over "nasty carpet," or the idea of having an open concept, and a white-on-white kitchen are all concepts presented to us by what's available and who wants to sell it. Repetition of those messages creates permanency, and our brain accepts them as facts. Do you think you would make different design choices if all the generations of options were open to you without limitations or judgment?

Advertisers tell us what to believe. Here's a great example from an article in the New York Times:

"Fifty years ago, the sugar industry pointed our nation's declining health to fat, knowing they had a large part in it. The result was published in the New England Journal of Medicine in 1967."[1]

To this day, fat remains the bad guy and is often misunderstood.

So what's the fuss about? Advertisements, movies, games, and even the news all have the power to program what you believe to be true.

*There is opposition in all things*
*With every bad comes its opposite good.*

This book isn't about screen time being "bad"; it's about being aware of the positive and negative aspects and balancing them. It is how you regain control. It's all about repetition. When the subconscious is repeatedly bombarded with the same information, it will finally accept it as fact, whether it is true or not.

## Parental Concerns

So what makes screen time so threatening? Here are a few of the concerns parents, grandparents, teachers, and mentors have brought up.

- ISOLATION - In my own experience, my fourteen-year-old grandson literally locked himself away hour after hour, hiding from reality. If no one saw him, then they wouldn't bother him. He would quietly come out long enough to go to the bathroom and accept food donations. Even now, at seventeen, when not working or in school, he drifts back to solitude. It has been reported by the WebMD that kids ages eight to eighteen now spend seven hours and thirty-eight minutes plugged into media.

- ANGER AND AGGRESSION - Parents report that their children become irate whenever their screen time is interrupted or threatened. These reactions are amplified many times over from that same child's usual responses.
- PERSONALITY CHANGE - Many parents describe a Dr. Jekyll and Mr. Hyde type personality shift as children become more agitated, irritable, and aggressive.
- LACK OF PHYSICAL INTERACTION - We are social animals in need of positive touch and eye contact that communication through a screen does not provide. Without this, people become anxious and depressed.
- DECREASE IN PHYSICAL ACTIVITY - Children no longer run, play, climb trees, or create and imagine. The screen does it all, keeping them closed in and inactive.
- LACK OF FRESH AIR AND SUNSHINE - Our children's health is declining, and illnesses such as obesity and diabetes are on the rise. Our bodies need to move and explore the world

around us, inhale the fresh air, and absorb sunshine to activate vitamin D production. Are your children gray or ashen? Do they have dark circles under their sunken eyes? They need to get outside.

- SLEEPLESSNESS - Many parents complain that their child stays up throughout the night on their screens or has a restless night's sleep, then sleeps during class. It is during sleep that the mind resets, working through situations and problem-solving. The brain can't get closure when it is constantly bombarded with more information. It is also the time when most physical growth should happen.
- BRAIN DEVELOPMENT - Reports show that a child should not be exposed to screen time before a certain age due to possible developmental delays. Scientists are still discovering the effects of screen time on our young children. They have found that it seems to lower the development of white matter or "brain shrinkage" in teens and young adults.[2] You lose what you don't use. Our devices provide all the information we need. A child is no longer encouraged to imagine a

story or a consequence; it is presented to them. ADHD diagnoses have multiplied and appear at later ages.[3]

- FAILURE TO LAUNCH - This may seem like an unusual thing to worry about with a fourteen-year-old; however, research shows that the iGen generation (1995-2012) fails to engage in social interactions and lacks the desire to get a license and drive or get a job. They are unprepared for adulthood. On the other hand, they are less rebellious, less likely to get into brawls; they don't drink alcohol. And you don't have to worry about them coming home late after a date—they don't seem to do much of that either. Even though they seem to be living the life they want, they are not happy. Their identities live in cyberspace.[4]

- SOCIAL MEDIA HAS CHANGED SOCIAL INTERACTIONS - Many feel they can be more open and often hurtful when communicating from behind the screen. Blog.usejournal.com states, "Our addiction also ties into a need to find validation from others and the need to share our lives online, in the process neglecting our own happiness."[5] A good example might be the girl who finally gets to go to Disneyland but never sees or experiences any of it because she is totally lost in her phone.

- INCREASED EMOTIONAL INSTABILITY AND SUICIDE RATES - The fact that our children are increasingly becoming emotionally volatile has already come up several times. Anxiety and depression are common in our high schools to the point that our teens are being medicated. Being inexperienced, they cannot cope with the slightest bit of negative pressure, and teen suicide rates are rising drastically.

- INAPPROPRIATE CONTENT - With as much time as our children are connected to their screens, we wonder what they are being taught. Does the screen's information align with our family values? Today's cartoons are a good example. Have you banned certain shows due to violence, inappropriate language or for teaching tricks to best bully, or sexual content that is inappropriate for our young viewers?

- ADDICTION–BOTH PHYSICAL AND EMOTIONAL - As we notice the

personality changes and the anger taking away a device from our children for any reason, we must wonder are they addicted? Are these devices capable of causing a physical addiction? Is it more than just a game or a way to stay in contact with each other?

- CYBERBULLYING & PREDATORS - As the percentage of time spent online increases, so does the opportunity to be bullied. It also makes it possible for the predators to find your child. It has always been a challenge to be accepted in the school hierarchy. Bullying from behind the screen seems safer for the bully and they don't have to address the consequences of being seen.[6]

These concerns can make us feel fearful and anxious because we only see the worst scenarios. When we are in this state of mind, our thinking becomes reactive and jaded; we may feel like we need to control every moment and everyone to protect or fix them.

**Workbook 4A: Concerns or Fears Regarding Your Children and Screen Time**

- Please take a moment to list your concerns or fears regarding your children and screen time, and, for every concern, also answer: Why do I feel threatened by this? Knowing this, you can focus on discovering what you need to make an informed decision and action step.

_____

_____

_____

_____

_____

_____

_____

_____

_____

_____

_____

_____

_____

_____

_____

_____

## UNIQUE TO YOU (Use these lines for extra notes or to strategize.)

_____

_____

_____

_____

_____

_____

_____

_____

_____

_____

_____

_____

_____

_____

_____

_____

# 5  FINDING THE POWER WITHIN YOU

When my boys were young, they loved to watch He-Man as he raised his sword in the air, shoulders back, legs standing firm, and declared, "I have the power!"

You don't have to be a superhero to find the power within you.

Believing that you can make a difference is where you start. Becoming aware of the threat or concern is next. Knowing what that threat entails and eliminating it is essential, but your ability to find the strength to act and see it through is your superpower. You have been given this unique ability to do just that. Discovering where and how these fantastic powers can serve you will provide you with the success you are looking for. Taking on screen time will require that you have both the information and support, especially when confronting yourself.

## Maslow's Hierarchy of Needs

Are you aware of Maslow's Hierarchy of Needs? Psychologist Abraham Maslow theorized that first, we need life's basics: food, water, and shelter. We can't move forward without meeting them because we're too busy staying alive to focus on anything else. Once we have this in place, we can focus on safety, including shelter, clothing, security, and being protected from danger. Imagine going camping and roughing it. Not until all these needs are in place can you stop and relax around the fire and enjoy belonging—the third level, which includes being a part of a family or group where we feel acceptance and love. As we overcome various challenges, we develop self-esteem, reaching the fourth level.

The fifth and highest level in Maslow's hierarchy of needs is self-actualization, where we accept higher laws of morality, acceptance, less judgment, and are free to express our creativity. We become confident, receive respect, and respect others. We find ways to help others work their way up the hierarchy.

The truth is that we bounce between these levels as life moves forward. Think back to how you responded to the changes the COVID-19 pandemic quarantines placed on all of us. Suddenly, we were struggling in the first two levels of basic needs and safety. This is simply a part of life's journey.

The fourth level, esteem, tells us that not only do we need to be accepted, but we need to be valued. It is why we often make crazy decisions, like eating food we know will make us miserable, or needing to maintain a social presence and receive feedback on social media, no matter the cost.

Failing at any of these levels is a severe blow to our self-esteem. Now that we have our phones and other devices, we have an option: "If I can't find my value in the real world, I'll just create my own." So here we sit, stuck bouncing between needs back and forth, and those who can't find their place run from life entirely, depressed, anxious, and suicidal. In my book, *The Future is Mine to Design*[1], I suggest that five pillars or beliefs need to be in place in order to advance through Maslow's hierarchy of needs successfully. Here are three of them:

**Pillar #1** - THE ONLY CONSTANT IN LIFE IS CHANGE. Hold on to that belief as you move forward. Take action; it's only when you're in motion that each challenge guides you toward your next step, heading you into a future of your design.

**Pillar #2** - YOU ONLY HAVE COMPLETE CONTROL OVER YOURSELF. This step may be one of the hardest. I've gotten used to being allowed and even expected to make choices for others. Choosing to follow you is in your child's power. I'm sure you are painfully aware of the first time your young child told you "no." Accepting this changes the whole dynamic; you become a guide that teaches life's ground rules and allows others to govern themselves. You can't control and save everybody else. To gain self-control, we need to understand not just how we can gain control but why.

**Pillar #4** - THERE IS OPPOSITION IN ALL THINGS. Despite all the positive characteristics our amazing devices provide us with, there is a negative or harmful effect as well. Understanding this allows us to create balance.

## Regaining Control

Since children don't come with instruction manuals, and 'how to deal with our emotions' wasn't a subject taught in school, we've had to "fake it." We've learned through the examples of others who are also doing their best to get by. Without the information we need to understand how our mind works we often let our feelings control our next step. Fortunately, man has discovered more about our amazing mind and body and these experts are willing to share their knowledge so that we too can take control of our own lives.

## Triggers

The classic knee-jerk reaction or "trigger" begins with ACTIONS that elicit EMOTIONS that provoke REACTIONS. As we go through life, we collect experiences and then translate them into programs. The more we repeat each program, the more set or automatic it becomes.

For example: ACTION—your kids fight over a device; EMOTION—frustration, anger; REACTION—you take away the device. There is very little conscious thought. It's automated. Your only goal is to get the noise to stop. What if we could break the cycle just long enough to act more rationally, more consciously?

In the confidence heart image at the beginning of this chapter, you can follow the path as an adverse action triggers the brainstem, immediately releasing hormones like epinephrine (fight or flight) and cortisol, the stress hormone. You feel overwhelmed, anxious, angry, or scared. At this moment, you are unable to think clearly; you simply act—a classic knee-jerk reaction. What if you could stop and wait for the hormones to diffuse, then the information that upset you would have time to travel to the frontal lobe where the executive function takes place, and you could think it through before acting.

## Pattern Interrupts

"Pattern interrupts" are techniques that give you the time you need to think more clearly and rationally. Here are a few examples. You can come up with your own that works for you.

- Close your eyes and take a deep breath, then slowly exhale. Deep breathing helps to decrease the cortisol or stress hormone. It relaxes your muscles and allows you to focus.
- The Five-Second Rule: Mel Robbins is the author of *The 5 Second Rule: Transform your Life, Work, and Confidence with Everyday Courage.*[2] She suggests that once you recognize the trigger, you stop, then slowly count backward from five to zero, interrupting the impulse to act just long enough to

allow conscious thought. When using this technique, *you* can decide how best to react and not let the old programming control you.

- Parent Time Out: This is an amazing privilege we never stop to think we have. When we are forced into a stressful situation, such as coping with fighting with a child over their screen time use, we find ourselves lost in the negative energy around that solution on the spot. Instead, stop and allow yourself time to calm down and think things through. You can even create a physical signal, like the time-out signal used in football. If it's your first time trying this, take a breath and let your child know that you need a moment but will return within a time period. Return with a decision and a reason for your decision. This could include needing more time to research or discuss the issue with your significant other. Your responsibility is to return in a timely fashion with a solution. This should be no longer than twenty-four hours.

## Workbook 5A: Parent Time Out

Sometimes, we are so overwhelmed and require more time to think things through. Develop a signal or statement that indicates you need some time to process the best solution, and that you will be back within a certain amount of time.

- Record your Parent Time Out signal and experience using it. Was it helpful?

_____

_____

_____

_____

_____

_____

_____

_____

_____

_____

_____

_____

_____

_____

_____

_____

_____

_____

_____

**Workbook 5B: Triggers**

Take two to three days to notice and record your triggers and how you felt.

For each trigger, answer the following:

- What triggered you?

_____

_____

_____

_____

_____

- What was the emotion it provoked?

_____

_____

_____

_____

_____

_____

- What pattern interrupt technique did you use—breathing, five-second rule, parent time out, or some combination?

_____

_____

_____

_____

_____

_____

- How did you react after using a pattern-interrupt?

_____

_____

_____

_____

_____

_____

_____

- What would your knee-jerk reaction have
  been?

_____

_____

_____

_____

_____

_____

_____

_____

_____

_____

## Becoming Self-Aware

Another way to better connect with your family is taught in the book *Leadership and Self-Deception: Getting Out of the Box.*[3] In this book, various authors share a technique that boosted their company's profits through the roof. Their secret? Respect and perspective. Think of the following as if you are the CEO of your family.

The authors first teach about in-the-box thinking. When you are in the box, you see others as objects that need to be moved and manipulated to adjust to what you want or need. Can you see the emotions and attitudes you are sharing with this type of thinking? You are more critical, short-tempered, and demanding.

When you choose to work out-of-the-box, you see those around you as people, each with their own experiences, perceptions, and needs. You still remain in control, but with a broader expectation for yourself and others. A simple mental question before you act, "Am I in or out of the box?", may help tweak your next action step as you move on. Your family members will be less rebellious when they feel they are seen and understood.

## Workbook 5C: Out-of-the-Box Thinking

Spend a day paying attention to how you act and react to those around you and how you respond to them. You can read more about this activity in the Intentional Communication Consultants article, "Is Self-Deception Keeping You in the Box?"[4]

- Make a list or a simple tally sheet of when you are "in the box" (seeing others as objects and moving them around to serve yourself) or "out of the box" (seeing them as individuals with their own stories and needs).

_____

_____

_____

_____

_____

_____

_____

_____

_____

_____

# BALANCING FAMILY SCREEN TIME

- Is there a difference in how you interacted with others or how they responded to you? Did cooperation increase or decrease?

---

---

---

---

---

---

---

---

---

---

---

---

---

---

---

---

---

## How Do I Know If I'm Addicted to My Phone?

In his book, *What's the Big Deal About Addictions?: Answers and Help for Teens*, James J. Crist, Ph.D., lists these signs of screen addiction:[5]

- You feel a need to respond immediately to any messages you get.
- You constantly check your phone even when it doesn't ring or vibrate.
- You feel anxious or depressed when you can't use your phone.
- You ignore what is going on around you to focus on your phone.
- If adults take your phone as punishment, you go to great lengths to get it back.
- Your grades drop because you spend more time on your phone than doing your homework or studying.
- Your neck aches because you are bending your head to look at your phone.
- You text or otherwise use your phone while driving, even though you know it's illegal, dangerous, and increases your chances of having an accident.

**Workbook 5D: Highlight the Signs of Addiction**

Refer to the above bullet point list of signs of screen addictions. Highlight, circle, or underline any of the bullet points that you can relate to.

## Becoming Aware of Your Personal Device Use

You are reading this book, which means you have concerns and are actively seeking answers. The following exercise is not a judgment, but a collection of evidence to convince your subconscious that changes may have to be made to keep you and your family safe and comfortable. Don't be afraid to be completely honest with yourself.

**Workbook 5E: Awareness**

Spend a few days or a week becoming aware of what devices you use and how long you use them.

- Record your findings below in your own Screen Time Tracking Sheet. Don't be hard on yourself. Play your first week out as best as you can. NO JUDGEMENT! You're just trying to sort things out. Nobody's perfect. Be aware that around day three, your mind will start challenging you. Don't get discouraged. Push your way through.

| Day 1 | |
|---|---|
| Device(s) used | |
| What did you use each device for? (watching TV, texting, scrolling on social media, playing a game, etc.) | |
| Time spent on each activity | |
| Total daily screen time | |

| Day 2 | |
|---|---|
| Device(s) used | |
| What did you use each device for? (watching TV, texting, scrolling on social media, playing a game, etc.) | |
| Time spent on each activity | |
| Total daily screen time | |

| Day 3 | |
|---|---|
| Device(s) used | |
| What did you use each device for? (watching TV, texting, scrolling on social media, playing a game, etc.) | |
| Time spent on each activity | |
| Total daily screen time | |

| **Day 4** | |
|---|---|
| Device(s) used | |
| What did you use each device for? (watching TV, texting, scrolling on social media, playing a game, etc.) | |
| Time spent on each activity | |
| Total daily screen time | |

| Day 5 | |
|---|---|
| Device(s) used | |
| What did you use each device for? (watching TV, texting, scrolling on social media, playing a game, etc.) | |
| Time spent on each activity | |
| Total daily screen time | |

| Day 6 | |
|---|---|
| Device(s) used | |
| What did you use each device for? (watching TV, texting, scrolling on social media, playing a game, etc.) | |
| Time spent on each activity | |
| Total daily screen time | |

| Day 7 | |
|---|---|
| Device(s) used | |
| What did you use each device for? (watching TV, texting, scrolling on social media, playing a game, etc.) | |
| Time spent on each activity | |
| Total daily screen time | |

## Overwhelm!

You have learned so much and worked so hard; congratulations on all your efforts. I promise it will be worth it in the end.

To give you an extra hand, I will reveal the fifth and final pillar from my book, *The Future is Mine to Design*:[6]

**Belief in Something Greater than Yourself.**

We can label it in whatever way we'd like—God, Jesus Christ, a saint, Buddha, Shiva, Allah, or you may choose the belief in crystals. When you choose to believe in something greater than yourself, you are fortified and are no longer alone. You believe your journey is supported and that you are loved and guided through it. You pray, knowing someone is not only listening, but stretching out their hand of support and guidance. The poem "Footsteps in the Sand"[7] shares this belief beautifully. This is a challenging journey, but one worth taking to reach your goal of building a better life for you and your family.

Pillars/Beliefs:

The only constant is change.
> You only have the power to change yourself.
> There's opposition in all things.
> Believe in something greater than yourself.

**UNIQUE TO YOU (Use these lines for extra notes or to strategize.)**

_____

_____

_____

_____

_____

# 6  YOU GO FIRST

I watched a video on Facebook of an eight-year-old boy tasked with feeding his little sister. This darling little Asian girl with a pixie haircut anxiously waits with her mouth wide open, ready for her next tasty bite, desperately tries to catch the spoon as it sways tauntingly back and forth in front of her mouth. Engrossed in his phone, her brother is entirely oblivious to her dilemma. Her frustration becomes clear as she freezes in place, scowling deeply. She has had enough and will take no more of this torture. Our little sweetheart reaches across the table, grabs the phone from her brother's hand, and drops it into a bin next to her. He looks at her stunned, almost surprised that she was even there.

It's time for self-reflection. Have you ever been guilty of ignoring your child or others because you were too engrossed in your phone or tablet? I have felt an instant wave of pure rage surge through me when someone has interrupted me. "How dare you disturb my swiping and scrolling, my dopamine rush?" The pressure explodes, lashing out at its nearest victim. Even as I realize my mistake and try to temper my reaction, my tone and body language send a distinct message, and that anger enters my enemy's soul.

How many times have you been completely engaged in a conversation while someone stares at their device? You get the message that nothing is more important than whatever is on their screen. Why would anyone take that personally? I'm sure you get my point, and I'm guilty as charged. Focusing on ourselves, we have to address how we relate to our devices and the people around us before expecting others to change their screen time habits.

What do your children see you do? Once, my grandson and I were at a small amusement park. He loves driving go-karts. While driving around the track, a young girl, lost in her phone, broadsided him. I wondered why she thought it was a good idea to even have her phone with her.

We are constantly taking in information from our environment and processing it. Do we still fit within our cultural expectations? Whether or not you think that you matter, the truth is you and your actions have distinct impacts on those around you. Mirroring gives someone else instant permission to do the same thing you're doing, whether it's good or bad. It's time to become aware of yourself.

## Foundational Beliefs

Now that you're more aware of your screen time habits, you can decide if you want to take action and what it will be. My first step to recovery was to change what I believed. I discovered the sad truth that my foundational belief was this:

"My phone is my first priority in my life at all times!"

When I put it this way, I felt ashamed and wondered how it even became a thing. This program was no longer serving me. It was disrupting my routine and the way I interacted with my family and others. I realized that no matter what I was doing, if the phone rang, I would stop everything to answer it. I could be talking to someone I love, in the middle of doing something important, or even driving, and the phone couldn't wait. This had to stop. The world won't stop spinning, and I have proof.

In the "olden days," when our phones were at the other end of the house or ringing mysteriously under a pile of clothes, it took time to get to it. Believe me when I tell you it wasn't the end of the world, and it still isn't. If it were that important, they would call back or leave a message.

It was not just the physical habit of picking up the phone, it was also my unconscious need for my next dopamine hit. Every time our phones signal, it elicits the release of dopamine, the feel-good hormone, and we crave it so much that we ask for likes and make posts frequently, hoping for a response. The drug itself and our base need to be seen, validated, and accepted pulls us back into our phones and devices. I felt it deeply.

As you can see, changing any of my phone habits would be challenging. I needed to regain control over my life.

I challenged myself to ignore the phone until it was safe or free to answer at my leisure. I admit that the temptation to pick it up when it rings still elicits a slight hand jerk or my heart skips a beat, but then I remember, I'm in charge, not that stupid device. So I deleted my old program and wrote a new one, a simple declaration:

"I refuse to be a slave to my phone and other electronic devices."

I created a new foundational belief system that

better serves me and those around me. I built action steps based on this belief. I made signs reinforcing this declaration and posted them everywhere. Each time I saw one, I would speak the words out loud repeatedly, convincing my subconscious that I was serious about changing my programming. Now, I have greater control.

## How Can a Small Sentence Make Such a Difference?

You have already made several mental changes that are driving you forward. Let's add the last two pillars to your foundation[1].

Pillar #1: Change is the only constant in life.
Pillar #2: You only have complete power over yourself.
**Pillar #3: There is energy in all things.**
Pillar #4: There's opposition in all things.
**Pilar #5: Believe in something greater than yourself.**

"Water has memory" is a familiar phrase from the *Frozen* movie series. Our screens use energy and Wi-Fi. We are aware of light and sound waves. You feel that special something when you look into the eyes of someone you love and can distinctly feel the negative energy being thrown at you by an adversary. Music can rev you up or calm you down. There is energy in everything we touch, smell, taste, and especially in the words we speak.

I was attending a 3KeyElements[2] conference with Kirk Duncan when he shared an experiment with us. He told us that he took leftover rice, put it in two bottles, yelled at one and spoke kind words to the other. After a week, he checked to find that the rice that was yelled at was moldy and gross while the rice in the love jar remained white. It made absolutely no sense to me. So I had to try it out for myself. To my surprise, the rice in my love jar remained white and fluffy, and had grown light, airy, white mold. The rice in the hate jar was shriveled and grey and covered in black mold. Still to this day, this result amazes me. Later Dr. Emoto added a third jar that he completely ignored, this rice shriveled and dried up. So, what made the difference? Why didn't both jars of rice just decompose as expected?

In a world where we have to see to believe, we can watch Dr. Emoto's water experiments. His results will amaze you—water spoken to with simple words or short phrases creates different crystal formations when frozen. Positive comments created beautiful delicate crystals, whereas dark words formed dark globby masses. The words we hear and say give off a specific sound wave that the water in our bodies reacts to, creating a physical reaction that elicits an emotional response. The bottom line here is that what we hear and then feel determines how we respond. Words and sounds reinforce the message your subconscious receives and are instantly programmed into your belief system. What we say and how we say it sends a more profound message than just the words themselves. Be conscious of this as you approach your family. Choose your words wisely, and your success will multiply.

## Workbook 6A: Rice Experiment

Have some fun with your family and try the rice experiment. Your kids will want to prove you wrong. All the instructions are listed below or on YouTube.[3] You can check out how words affect water crystals on YouTube[4] as well. What do you think happened that made the jars of identical rice react differently? Have fun!

Instructions:

- To eliminate doubt, set up each sample in precisely the same way using three glass jars. Label one jar "LOVE"; one jar

"HATE"; and leave the third jar with no marker.

- To each of the jars, add either leftover rice, all from the same batch, or dry rice. Add water to the uncooked rice to cover. Tighten the lids down.
- When I did this experiment, I took an extra precaution because I didn't want the sounds around the house to affect the experiment. I took the "LOVE" jar down the hall and spoke to it lovingly. I told it how grateful I was for the nutrition it gives us, how beautiful it was, etc. Then I placed it in the back of my closet. I got the "HATE" jar, walked down the hall yelling at it, told it how worthless, hard, and dry it was, etc. I placed it next to the "LOVE" jar. At this time, I didn't have a third jar. I left them alone for about a week.

Love is amazing and powerful. Hate is harsh and demeaning, but at least you're being seen. But you are nothing, nobody, the cruelest life of all when you are ignored. Be conscious of this as you approach your family. Choose your words wisely, and your success will follow.

- Reflect on your experience.

Ready-Set-Go

Since you already made a list of your device habits in the last chapter, you too can choose one or two of them that you may want to upgrade, but keep it simple and develop a new foundational belief that you will build your action steps on, such as, "I do not have to stop everything and answer my phone!" Write your phrase on paper and place them around your home, office, or car. Repeat your thought each time you see it.

## Workbook 6B: Build a New Foundational Belief

- What was your old foundational belief? (Example: My phone has priority in my life at all times!)

_____

_____

_____

_____

_____

_____

_____

- What is your new foundational belief? (Example: I refuse to be a slave to this small object.)

_____

_____

_____

_____

_____

_____

_____

Creating a new foundational belief statement and repeating it often is a giant step towards success. Post it and repeat it often.

Now it is time to create action steps that align with your new foundational belief.

Action step suggestions:

- Look up and make eye contact whenever you speak to someone or when others talk to you. How do you think your interactions will change? Would you expect it to be a more positive or more negative experience? What message are you sending when you make this change? On YouTube, there is a video about "looking up."[5]

- Choose to put your phone on airplane mode or the "do not disturb while driving" option. If you absolutely need to use your phone, wait until you have safely pulled over.

- Charge your phone outside your bedroom. Studies show that your body is still on the alert for the subsequent notification or text and cannot shut down completely when your phone is in your room overnight. This means your mind never gets to shut down and recharge. Even a computer needs time to stop, reset, and upgrade. No wonder you're still tired when it's time to get up.

## Workbook 6C: Action Steps

Choose one or two habits from your Screen Time Tracking Sheet from the Workbook 5E section that you'd like to upgrade and create the action steps you'll need to make it happen.

Once you've chosen your action step (Example: I

will place my phone on my not-while-driving setting and pull over if I need to use the phone in an emergency), answer the accompanying questions below before you put it into practice. It's time to convince your brain that you're serious about this.

- Write down your action step(s) and the amount of time you need to put it in place. This will allow you to re-evaluate your actions and adjust as needed.

_____

_____

_____

_____

_____

_____

- Why did you choose this action step? Answering this question reinforces your "why" to your subconscious.

_____

_____

_____

_____

_____

_____

_____

_____

_____

_____

- What do you already have in place to
  make this happen? Realizing what you've
  already done provides encouragement
  —"Hey, this idea is not so far-fetched
  after all"—and is another way to reinforce
  this change to your subconscious.

_____

_____

_____

_____

_____

_____

_____

_____

_____

_____

_____

_____

_____

_____

_____

_____

- What else do you still need to do to accomplish your goal? This will provide clarification and instructions for your subconscious to search for the answers you need.

_____

_____

_____

_____

_____

_____

_____

_____

Remember, your desires have a lot of competition with many of your established programs or habits. You are literally fighting a battle between your body/established programs and your soul/the desire to take back control, build, and grow. Giving your subconscious the most information possible lets it know you're serious.

Your mind will challenge you as soon as three days. Become aware especially if you're slipping. Repeat your foundational belief and action step and remind your subconscious that this is what you want.

Repetition, repetition, repetition is what will set your new programs. Recording your actions daily on paper or in excel, for instance, will give you that extra punch you need to create those new neuropathways. Be sure to give yourself credit for all your positive actions. That's what your tracking sheet will help you see. Fortunately, it will also show you where you feel weak. Don't be afraid to admit it.

## Magic Trick #1

Give yourself permission not to be perfect. It is simply an indicator allowing you to adjust and tweak your action steps, encouraging forward movement. Many baby steps are much more effective than one giant leap.

. . .

**Workbook 6D: Action Step Tracker**

Use the action step tracker below to track your progress. No judgment! You're just trying to sort things out. Nobody's perfect. Remember to celebrate every small success.

Here is an example of an action step tracker:

**Goal: No Phone Use While Driving**

Week 1

| Action Steps: | Hands-free only | No reading/responding to texts | Use not-while-driving option | Airplane mode |
|---|---|---|---|---|
| Sun | | | | |
| Mon | X | | | |
| Tues | | | | |
| Weds | | 1 | | |
| Thurs | X | 2 | | |
| Fri | | 4 | | |
| Sat | | 1 | | |

## Week 2

| Action Steps: | Hands-free only | No reading/responding to texts | Use not-while-driving option | Airplane mode |
|---|---|---|---|---|
| Sun | X | 1 | | |
| Mon | X | 3 | | |
| Tues | | | X | |
| Weds | X | | X | |
| Thurs | X | | X | |
| Fri | | | X | |
| Sat | X | | X | |

In this example, our driver realized it was easier not to use the phone while driving if he was unaware of the notifications. So, he chose to take advantage of the "Not While Driving" feature on his phone, adjusting his action step to achieve his goal.

If you find that the action step you chose is too big or ineffective, tweak it until you can achieve your goal. One option might be to set a smaller expectation, such as only use the not-while-driving option on shorter drives at first and work your way up. However, give yourself a time limit when using this option. Check your resolve at the end of the week, then tweak and adjust. Make the first step challenging but doable. You'll be glad you overcame it, becoming the example you, your children, and others need.

Try it yourself:

- First, define your goal in the space below.

_____

_____

_____

_____

_____

_____

- Now, fill in the following tables with your actions steps and track how you do.

# Week 1

| Action steps: | | | | |
|---|---|---|---|---|
| Sun | | | | |
| Mon | | | | |
| Tues | | | | |
| Weds | | | | |
| Thurs | | | | |
| Fri | | | | |
| Sat | | | | |

# Week 2

| Action steps: | | | | |
|---|---|---|---|---|
| Sun | | | | |
| Mon | | | | |
| Tues | | | | |
| Weds | | | | |
| Thurs | | | | |
| Fri | | | | |
| Sat | | | | |

# Week 3

| Action steps: | | | | |
|---|---|---|---|---|
| Sun | | | | |
| Mon | | | | |
| Tues | | | | |
| Weds | | | | |
| Thurs | | | | |
| Fri | | | | |
| Sat | | | | |

## Week 4

| Action steps: | | | | |
|---|---|---|---|---|
| Sun | | | | |
| Mon | | | | |
| Tues | | | | |
| Weds | | | | |
| Thurs | | | | |
| Fri | | | | |
| Sat | | | | |

## Week 5

| Action steps: | | | | |
|---|---|---|---|---|
| Sun | | | | |
| Mon | | | | |
| Tues | | | | |
| Weds | | | | |
| Thurs | | | | |
| Fri | | | | |
| Sat | | | | |

**Workbook 6E: Adjust Your Action Steps**

You can't decide if or what you want to change if you don't understand how you're spending your screen time. Go back over your Screen Time Tracking Sheet from the Workbook 5E section and reflect below:

- Which activities move you towards your goal of reconnecting with your family?

_____

_____

_____

_____

_____

_____

- Are there times when your screen time moves you in the opposite direction? These may be some options that you can use as action steps.

_____

_____

_____

_____

_____

_____

Magic Trick #2

Utilize the power of gratitude. As frustration rises and you begin to question your decision, stop. List five things you are grateful for to remind yourself how good you have it.

## Workbook 6F: Create an Attitude of Gratitude

- Journal/Record five things you are grateful for every day. This fills the soul. Your subconscious wants to believe it's doing something right, especially while we're asking it to change. When things get tough, add five more and breathe. You've got this! Start with your first five here.

_____

_____

_____

_____

_____

_____

_____

After you have slain a few of your own dragons, you can decide when you're ready to move on and involve your family. Don't forget to celebrate along the way. You're doing so well.

**UNIQUE TO YOU (Use these lines for extra notes or to strategize.)**

_____

_____

_____

_____

_____

_____

_____

_____

_____

_____

_____

_____

_____

# 7 PARENTING, REWARDS, AND CONSEQUENCES

Positive reinforcement is a powerful reward, whether it occurs organically or deliberately. When your mind is rewarded for doing a good job, it is much more likely to repeat that same action. A dose of serotonin or even dopamine is a positive reward encouraging you to repeat your activity over and over again.

Our children didn't come with instruction manuals. Fortunately, there are parenting experts that will supply these guidelines for you. We each learn in our own way. Here are three different teaching-style resources I have enjoyed. See if one of them speaks to you.

- Nicholeen Peck is called the Self-Government Lady.[1] She teaches positive parenting techniques that help build the foundation for your children to govern themselves.[2]

- Dr. Paul Jenkins from Live on Purpose shares his knowledge relating to positive parenting in his own unique way.[3]
- Foster Cline is famous for his book, *Parenting with Love and Logic*.[4]

Nicholeen Peck teaches that the first thing parents need to teach is how to follow instructions[5], which aligns with Dr. Paul Jenkins' "stages of maturity."[6] If your child is not in a place where they can follow instructions, they are operating at a Stage 1 maturity level that cannot cooperate or be reasoned with. In this stage, emotions are running the show without rhyme or reason.

## Five Steps of Following an Instruction

Nicholeen's five steps of following an instruction include:[7]

1. Look at the person giving the instruction
2. Have a calm face, voice, and body
3. Say okay or disagree appropriately
4. Do the task immediately
5. Check back

In any confrontation, it is important to understand that moving from a place of emotion to calmness should be your priority rather than the infraction itself. We need to allow our children to process what triggered them and allow them to diffuse their emotions, thereby moving the thought from the back of the head toward the frontal lobe where they can now process what happened to the best of their ability. Of course, to accomplish this, we need to be in a calm space ourselves. Hopefully, you've been practicing your calming techniques/pattern interrupts from chapter 5. However, creating a new foundational belief related to this situation could be very helpful as well.

My first child had severe colic and cried all the time. I can't say I wasn't frustrated and tired as I paced back and forth throughout the night to keep her calm, but I did understand that she wasn't being malicious or doing it to annoy me. I realized it wasn't her fault. With that foundational belief in place, anger and frustration dissipated, and I paced as a gift of love.

It is a common misconception that your child processes the situation the way you do. This is completely untrue. All our reasoning comes from a lifetime of past experiences, which they haven't had yet. The only way to fix this is to create a new foundational belief:

Instead of: "My child doesn't think or reason like a grown up."

Think: "When my child is in Stage 1, I understand they are being controlled by their emotions; they are impulsive and unable to process the situation clearly."

Warning! Never make any judgments or create consequences until you are both calm! Stop and reset. Reprove or teach with love.

## Workbook 7A: Create a Foundational Belief For When Your Child Is Overwhelmed by an Emotion

Create a new foundational belief for when your child is operating in Stage 1 (being controlled by their emotions). For example, when my child is in Stage 1, I will:

- Close my eyes and take a deep breath to place myself in a calm place.
- Give the time-out signal, letting them know I understand where they are coming from, but I can't help them until they become calm.
- Allow my child to release their emotions without causing physical or emotional pain to others. They may need to take a

time-out, yell at a tree, or run around the backyard ten times, for example. Once they are ready, they can return and ask if you are ready to talk.

- Once you are both calm, it is essential to discuss what triggered them and why. Perhaps you can find a solution that will be agreeable to both of you. You will need to teach these new rules by example and simple instructions the first few times.

Being able to follow instructions is a sign that our children are operating in Stage 2 of Jenkins' levels of maturity.[8] In this stage, when they are more open to discuss and help decide on consequences, we need to understand what we consider following instruction.

- Now, you try. Complete the following sentence.

*When my child is operating in Stage 1, I will .
. .*

_____

_____

_____

_____

_____

## Consequences

Consequences are a natural part of life. You climb a tree and step on a weak branch; it breaks, you fall. You eat too much candy; you get a stomachache and cavities. You don't turn in your homework; your grade drops. These are natural consequences. Allow and guide your child to problem-solve these issues independently. Unless they are at risk of physical harm, let them fall so they can learn how to get back up. It's the struggle that makes them stronger, more flexible, and more capable adults.

We learn and grow by figuring out what works and what doesn't. Without consequences, there would be no discoveries or inventions, no fancy phones or devices. Too much time on our devices causes personality and mood changes. These consequences are what drive us to find balance. All consequences are meant to teach, not punish. When used with love and pure intent, consequences will direct us to the next lesson or experience. Consequences are an opportunity for you and your child to grow and should never be used to manipulate, hurt, or get back at someone. Here are a few guidelines:

- Allow yourself time to diffuse your emotion by using the Five Second Rule.
- Before speaking, quickly remind yourself

which teaching style or language your child speaks.

- Be calm and smile. Speak softly and in a non-judgmental way. Once you have chosen the action steps, rewards, and consequences together, simply repeat the offense and the consequences you all decided upon as a family.
- When both you and your child know the rules, there is less drama because it is predictable. Stay consistent! For example, a consequence might be to give a child a simple age-appropriate chore, allowing them time to calm down and process the event. Once the task is finished, the consequence is complete, and the weight is lifted.
- Remember to balance the offense with the punishment. Not all crimes are capital offenses.
- Remember Stage 1 children are unable to comply at this time. Focus on defusing the emotions. If they need a time out, they should find a calm place to regroup without distractions or benefits. Allow them the time they need but be sure this issue is resolved as soon as possible.
- Stage 2 children want to resolve the

conflict. State the infraction and the consequence. These children want to resolve the issue quickly and painlessly so they can get on with what they're doing.

## Workbook 7B: Create an Initial Consequences List

Begin by watching Dr. Jenkins' *How to Come Up With Good Consequences* video on YouTube.[9]

You can also check out these two other videos to help with creating consequences:

- *Setting Consequences For Teenagers* from Nicholeen Peck.[10]

- *Why Are Consequences An Important Part Of Positive Parenting* from Dr. P. Jenkins.[11]

- Now, create an initial consequences list. You will add more once your family is involved.

_____

_____

_____

_____

_____

_____

_____

_____

_____

_____

_____

_____

_____

_____

_____

_____

_____

_____

_____

_____

_____

_____

_____

_____

_____

_____

## Tracking Positive Behavior

Before we talk about rewards or alternate activities, you need to decide how you will track your child's positive behavior. I use simple tally marks hourly or fill a jar with beans. It doesn't matter how you keep track; it only matters that you keep track and give the rewards earned. You know how your family operates, and they can help add their own ideas when you get together to discuss these changes.

## Workbook 7C: Decide How You Will Track Positive Behavior

Choose how you will track the "points" that your children earn for promised rewards.

Dr. Jenkins talks about using red chips.[12] Three red chips result in a consequence, the loss of points, giving your child a warning, or a stop break. This works best for children in Stage 1.

I used simple tally marks hourly and assigned a value to "X" amount of marks.

You know how your family operates. Ask your family members for ideas.

- How will you track positive behavior?
  Write it down.

_____

_____

_____

_____

_____

_____

_____

_____

_____

_____

_____

_____

_____

_____

_____

_____

## Rewards & Alternate Activities

Alternate activities is a list of options your child has when they're off screen time. It is only fair that we help fill that space for them initially. They've literally forgotten the options they have available to them. I found that after I helped a few times, my grandchildren suddenly remembered the activities they used to do and now plan what they want to do instead. There are times now that they spend more time off than on their devices. You can also use these activities as a part of your reward system.

I have often found myself in a place where I wish I had a reward of some kind on hand, and it's often difficult to think of something at the last minute. The truth is, sometimes, I just don't want to randomly stop and bake cookies or do a science experiment. With that being said, if I plan and have the things I need for several fancier rewards or activities available, I am more prepared mentally to take on larger projects. I know when the kids are getting close to having earned enough points for a reward, so I have no excuses not to be committed and ready to spend the time with them as promised.

We love to make videos and occasionally do random Facebook lives. One time, we tried to see if an egg would cook in the hot tub if we kept it in there long enough. Silly, but fun, and it was an experiment that took several days. (By the way, no, the egg didn't even begin to cook, but it did absorb the chlorine from the water.)

Have rewards like cookies or candy on hand. I keep simple mixes or recipes and their ingredients on my shopping list and in my pantry. So often, a troubled child will find himself while cooking. They are able to accomplish something, and the reward is something yummy to eat. Sometimes, a quick trip to Wendy's for a small Frosty is also fun.

Finding something the whole family enjoys can be tricky, but you can agree to take turns when choosing the next group activity. Someone will always disagree, so stick to your guns and know that even the toughest nut will crack.

Any small sign of cooperation, even things that seem unrelated to screen time, needs to be rewarded. Each person needs to feel seen and valued; otherwise, they will act the way they believe you see them, which is usually negative. You're building an environment of trust, so all rewards, praises, or simple kindness must be sincere. Look them in the eyes and touch their shoulders. Share your positive energy.

## Reward Guidelines

- Never use the word "but." For example, "You did very well, but . . ." This one word devalues your praise instantly. (Dr. P Jenkins)[13]

- Create a simple system like points on a board or beans in a jar.
- Choose the value of each mark or bean or how many they need to earn specific rewards.
- Plan on frequent small rewards to reinforce their positive cooperation, such as a smile, hug, or praise.
- Balance the value of the act to the value of the reward.
- Choose a timeline or a specific day they can cash out their rewards. Please don't leave them hanging. Stay consistent.
- Make their rewards age-appropriate, something they really want.
- Rewards can include tech time but be careful and be specific as to what that includes.
- Be willing to spend time with your children. Cooking, crafting, going to the park, or science projects are all fantastic rewards.
- Let your children add their ideas to the list. They can be very creative, and you may be surprised by what they come up with.

- Watch your budget. Time is also at a premium, keep that in mind as you plan your rewards.
- "Thank you for . . ." and "I'm proud of you because . . ." should be shared frequently.

## Workbook 7D: Family Reward System

- Make a list of rewards/alternate activities you think could work for you and your family. Have these reward options on hand. Set a time when you will have group activity time, then you and your family will be prepared. Don't let them down if at all possible. But if you do, be sure to apologize, reset the date, and follow through. You're building trust.

_____

_____

_____

_____

_____

_____

_____

_____

_____

_____

_____

_____

_____

_____

_____

If at any time you feel your rewards need to be tweaked, get together and make those adjustments as a family. When building trust, success is dependent on all of you working together.

**UNIQUE TO YOU (Use these lines for extra notes or to strategize.)**

_____

_____

_____

# BALANCING FAMILY SCREEN TIME

# 8 EVERY ROADBLOCK HAS A DETOUR

R oad construction is a common occurrence. It is frustrating, especially when it is unexpected. Almost every roadblock has suggested detours.

Making these changes in your life is a bold move on your part. Just recognizing the need and accepting it as true is one few people consider, let alone act on. You're amazing! To move toward your dream life, we need to put some guardrails in place for life's detours.

## Roadblock #1: Exhaustion and Stress

You're the foundation of your family, and you need to be strong yet flexible when an earthquake hits. Everything you do needs to point your family toward your goal while expecting a quality roller coaster ride on the way.

Parents often think they have to be superheroes and engaged at all times, fixing and saving the world. This is a lot of weight to carry and extremely exhausting. If you are reading this book, you are planning on making a considerable change that includes all your family members, plus some. It is essential that you take care of yourself. Without your steadfastness, your endeavor will fail. So make time to step away and remind yourself of the life you envisioned for your family's future. Schedule time for a nice long bath, time in nature and fresh air, or spend some time doing what you love, like scrapbooking or other activities, giving your body and mind time to recharge. It's not only a break, but a time for you to reward yourself. Be sure to celebrate knowing you can do hard things and that the goal you envision is entirely doable. Here are some other things you can do to take care of you:

- Focus on good food and quality sleep.
- Turn off your screen time an hour before you go to sleep and charge your phone in another room.
- Take quality supplements.
- Drink a gallon of water throughout the

day, and not so much pop, juice, etc. Save it for one of your rewards.

- Review your goals and the reasons you want to achieve them before going to bed. When you get up in the morning, gather all the wisdom your subconscious found for you and record it in a journal.
- Visualize by adding all your senses when you imagine what your life looks like in the future.
- Don't forget to give yourself credit for completing your action step tracker and celebrate. Look for those points that need tweaking and give yourself permission not to be perfect.

As you work toward your goal, don't use a cheat day as your reward. We don't want to lose ground just yet. My experience is that when we go back to our old habits, it is often very difficult to refocus and start again.

## Workbook 8A: Create a Vision Statement

Keep yourself strong and healthy physically and emotionally. Create a vision statement and action steps to support your great effort.

- Record your vision statement.

_____

_____

_____

_____

_____

_____

- What are your action steps?

_____

_____

_____

_____

_____

_____

_____

_____

_____

## Roadblock #2: Addressing Your Concerns with Your Partner

Expressing and discussing your concerns with your partner is vital to your success. Depending on your family dynamic, this could be problematic, especially if they are not entirely on board. You only have control over yourself. Remember any small step toward your goal is forward motion. Keep the following in mind when working with your partner:

- Show respect and acknowledge their right to choose.
- No talking behind their backs, especially when the children can hear.
- Accept any positive motion graciously.
- Accept that any discord between you will be taken advantage of by your children.
- Don't set your expectations too high.
- Build in action steps that balance out your roadblocks. If your significant other refuses to give up watching TV in the family room, then perhaps work on other rules—no phones at the dinner table or in the bathrooms, for example.
- Discuss your plans and explain why you're implicating these changes so that they can help reinforce your action steps.

Remember, they have the power to choose if they want to comply.

- Be the bigger person and an excellent example.

The rules you create apply to grandparents, aunts, uncles, or friends who visit your home. Hopefully, if they are aware and understand the limitations you have set, they will be able to back you up, but it is your responsibility to make that possible. For instance, when my grandson is grounded from tech, but no one warns me, I can't help. It's also an excellent time for the child to manipulate the situation. Don't set yourself up for that. Let others know what your rules are and why you're making these changes to prevent friction in the end; it's your house, your rules.

## Workbook 8B: Share Your Plans with Your Partner

- Discuss your plans with your significant other. How do they feel about these changes? Is there a way to compromise if they aren't fully onboard? Respect their right to choose. Record how your discussion goes.

- List each roadblock and describe the detour you took or can take in this situation.

_____

_____

_____

_____

_____

_____

_____

_____

_____

_____

_____

_____

_____

_____

## Workbook 8C: Set Limitations for Other Adults with Your Children

Figure out how you will deal with your new limitations when your children are in the care of other adults inside your home or theirs.

- Write your limitations here.

_____

_____

_____

_____

_____

_____

_____

_____

_____

_____

_____

_____

_____

## Roadblock #3: The Threat of Change

We all approach change in our own way. Let me give you an example. Once, my husband and I decided to start a diet. His take on this was to eat and enjoy everything he wanted while he could because tomorrow would come soon enough. I, on the other hand, had to start wrapping my head around it. So I did my best to learn and apply its principles to be ready and prepared by the time this lifestyle change began—two very different ways of approaching change.

Your family and friends are probably beginning to notice that something's up. They are going to ask questions and make some positive, but probably more negative, statements. They don't know what to think about the changes you're making. They liked you the way you were—predictable—and now, you're shaking things up. If I were your teenage daughter, I'd be worried: "What if my crazy mom starts messing with my phone?" Expect these reactions, and don't let them derail you. If you have an "S" personality, you might begin to question your resolve and cave. Don't! This is one of the many roadblocks you will grow through during your journey.

Watch those around you; remember to take into consideration their personality and stay outside the box. While they're trying to figure you out, it is a great time to collect intel on how each member re-acts. No matter who it is, they will need some time to absorb the change that is coming. Don't spill the beans just yet.

## Workbook 8D: Share Your Plans with Your Family

No doubt your family will notice the habits you've been changing. Now is a great time to teach why you are changing. Keep it casual unless they ask for more information.

- Record how your family reacts and what you've been able to share with them.

_____

_____

_____

_____

_____

_____

_____

_____

_____

## Getting Inside Your Child's Head

Discovering what is actually going on in your child's head and discovering what they are thinking and why they are doing what they do will give you a broader perspective. It will help you address issues from your child's point of view. Otherwise, you might be making assumptions and addressing the wrong problem. It is important to remember that our body language and tone give away our true feelings. Prepare to be open to whatever they have to say so that your child will learn that it's safe to share more openly. Take a deep breath, close your eyes, and shake off all negativities. Most importantly, smile and listen.

Every time we move toward change, it requires us to disassemble the familiar, making a gigantic mess. It's like cleaning out your closet. Only after you've pulled out everything and thrown out what no longer serves you are you free to put it back the way you want. Because of this, we need to shake things up in our world as we get deeply involved in discovering what kind of screen time our children are lost in.

This is meant to be very casual; ask questions about the storyline of a video game or what's happening in social media. The trick here is to be sincere and non-threatening. Your children will be surprised and possibly a little leery, but they may open up with continued interest as long as they don't feel judged.

## Trust Building

Remember these kids have been exposed to all types of media for a while now. Do not interrupt or turn off their gaming, etc. They need to learn to trust you. You haven't objected to this activity before, so don't start now. If this is a program you feel strongly about, please step back and consider all the pros and cons before taking action.

Your primary mission is to become aware of what's happening in your children's world and how they feel when they are playing or stop playing. It's important to show no signs of judgment. You are simply collecting intel. This may be a challenge at first, but you can do it. It's time to get involved with your children and the programs they are so lost in. The trick here is to:

- Show a genuine interest in what they are doing
- Ask questions without judgment
- Watch your tone
- No matter what they are watching, do not interrupt them!

You are building trust. A trust that will give them the freedom to talk to you freely in the future. Show continued interest without judgment. It takes time to gain their trust. Don't let fear get the best of you, and as mentioned above, DO NOT INTERRUPT OR STOP WHAT THEY ARE DOING! If necessary, after you've had time to process your emotions and thoughts, you can decide how to handle your concerns.

**Workbook 8E: Show Interest in Your Children's Technology Use**

Your goal is to become aware of what's happening in your children's world and how they feel when playing or when they stop playing, without judgment. They'll know if you're faking it, so do your best.

- Explore how the different types of screen time make them feel. Why do they need or want to play, what makes it so much fun, and how do they feel afterward?

_____

_____

_____

_____

_____

_____

_____

_____

_____

_____

_____

_____

- Take notes on which games/programs/social medias each child is using or playing. How do you feel about each one, and what are your concerns? Could any of these programs be used as a reward?

_____

_____

_____

_____

_____

- As you explore your child's screen time activity, stay consistent. Should your resolve weaken, don't belittle yourself; instead, see it as a time to explore. What triggered you? Were you feeling physically or emotionally vulnerable? Did an old fear or belief system creep out unexpectedly? Search, don't judge.

_____

_____

_____

_____

_____

_____

_____

_____

_____

_____

_____

_____

_____

- How does your child feel during and when not playing or watching?

Talking about screen time is challenging since your children instantly become defensive. It's often hard to find the right way to start these conversations. Using books and stories often opens those closed doors. Your child feels less threatened because the discussion is about a character in a book, and yet, the opportunity to teach and be taught becomes available.

Recently, with some of my grandchildren, we have been reading a middle grade-YA fiction called *Beyond Reality: The Lost*, a book I wrote with my grandson.[1] This story is about a thirteen-year-old boy who hides in his room, lost in his video games. One morning, after playing throughout the night, he finds himself inside his game. As he joins his hero, Tyrus, in search of the Heartstone to save his people, Dex quickly discovers that playing a game for real is nothing like playing it safely at home. Can you imagine the challenges Dex has to face living in this foreign world, fighting the enemy, and discovering that nothing is more important than family? We have had discussions that varied from being without the comforts of home to battling for freedom, equality, and of course, screen time.

This book is available both on Amazon as a paperback or ebook and on Audible. It comes with a program that includes comprehension and vocabulary, but also many activities and recipes for treats that support that book's message.

## Workbook 8F: Strategize How to Address Your Concerns

Now that you've had time to collect intel on how your children are spending their time on their devices, do you feel differently?

- List your concerns and possible ways to deal with them positively. You can use a character from a book, movie, or game to open a discussion without addressing a concern directly with your child. It's a great way to hear what they think.

_____

_____

_____

_____

_____

_____

_____

_____

_____

_____

**UNIQUE TO YOU (Use these lines for extra notes or to strategize.)**

_____

_____

_____

_____

_____

_____

_____

_____

_____

_____

_____

_____

_____

_____

_____

_____

# 9 FINDING YOUR WAY THROUGH THE ROADBLOCKS INSIDE YOU

How did you feel about being asked not to interrupt your child's time online while collecting information? Giving up control is a roadblock.

## Roadblock #4 Overcoming Your Own Beliefs and Emotions

Maintaining control of the world around us gives us a feeling of security. The foundational belief is, "I am in charge of my family's safety and health at all times. Any of their 'failures' are my responsibility." The action steps attached to this include staying aware and in control at all times.

Being in control doesn't mean that you are in the box and moving people around as you feel necessary for their safety. Instead, we have to step out of the box and see them as individuals growing through their experiences, good or bad. Our job is to love them unconditionally and guide them in a way that they can discover the answers for themselves.

So many of our young people haven't been given that opportunity because caring and well-intentioned parents have sheltered them from work, responsibility, and pain. We need a little more "tough love," which sounds negative, but it's not. It's only by experiencing and growing through the consequences of our actions that we learn and grow.

One of my favorite sayings is, "I didn't say it would be easy. I said it would be worth it."

## Workbook 9A: Reflect on Giving Up Control

- How did you feel about giving up control when you were asked not to interrupt your child's time online while collecting intel during workbook section 8E? Reflect here.

_____

_____

_____

Expect roadblocks and grow through them; set personal, and eventually family, rules that reinforce understanding and respect. Anyone involved in this change, including yourself, can become a roadblock. Of course, we're going to resist change. It's only natural. This detour will feel more like a maze and is trickier to maneuver since it's not just one roadblock but a series of them that keep moving, like the stairs at Hogwarts where each set of stairs moves, determined to throw you off track. You can think through possible solutions/action steps beforehand to help you work through it, reducing the scuffs and bumps you will find along the way.

Our feelings, opinions, and beliefs are often tied to old emotions or experiences, creating knee-jerk reactions. Are the concerns you've listed in 8F in your workbook still valid? Be honest with yourself. I had to give up the fear I felt about these devices, believing they were a threat to my grandchildren. I had to become open-minded enough to accept technology and create balance.

Another way to approach change is through a simple question, "What else could be true?" A very wise mentor loved to ask me that question, especially when I was fighting to justify my objections. That simple question stopped me in my tracks. I admit I resisted the idea at first, but as I explored other possibilities, true or not, my attitude softened.

As my grandson got ready to graduate from high school and enter the world of construction, my fears rose. How will the world's view change him? I feared the worst and made up all sorts of horror stories in my head. But when my mentor asked me once again, "What else could be true?" I was forced to see that this boy could thrive and grow through each experience and become the amazing man I always knew he could become.

## Workbook 9B: List Your Distractions or Roadblocks

- List your personal distractions or roadblocks. These can be mental, other people, or anything that may keep you from achieving the goal or action step you have set.

_____

_____

_____

_____

_____

_____

_____

_____

_____

_____

_____

_____

_____

_____

_____

- When you are tempted to react, stop, take a breath, and ask, "What else could be true?" Accept the ideas that come to you whether they are true or not. Did accepting these new ideas make a difference?

_____

_____

_____

_____

_____

_____

_____

_____

_____

_____

_____

_____

## Workbook 9C: Detours

- Describe the detour you could take or have already taken. Now, you'll be better prepared when these challenges present themselves.

_____

_____

_____

_____

_____

_____

_____

_____

_____

_____

_____

_____

_____

_____

_____

_____

_____

## Roadblock #5: Manage Your Expectations

You may have heard (or even experienced) the story of the wife who created a masterful meal to surprise her sweet husband, but he didn't come home until late due to unexpected problems at work. The food got cold, the candle melted, and she sat alone in a darkened room, heartbroken, and her expectations crushed. Dr. Jennice Vilhauer says, "Expectation plus action equals the creation of life experiences."[1]

Like the woman in this story, you too can have your expectations shattered, but not your soul. I have tried to gather my family with an expectation of comradery when instead, things have gone sideways, and their visit was nothing like I expected. I try to stay grounded, understanding that I have zero control over how others act. I can only control how I respond. Will I inflame the issue, or can I do my best to be the peacemaker and accept that despite it all, we are a family and that we love each other no matter what?

You know your family and realize that even with your best intentions and a finely tuned lesson plan, you may get to present only one thought. What would that one message be that begins the journey of your family joining you in balancing screen time? Remember, the why is more persuasive than the how. If you can create a no-tech zone at the dinner table or in the bathroom, you have succeeded. Even if all you get is complaints, you have opened the door and are still moving in the right direction. Remember to be patient, don't judge yourself, and be grateful for the progress you've made, one tiny baby step at a time. Your children will remember and appreciate your efforts, even if it's not until they have children of their own.

## Workbook 9D: Manage Expectations

Imagine the best results, the perfect family meeting.

Now imagine what it looks like at its worst. Expect something in the middle, whatever it is, and accept it as a success.

- Complete the following sentences.

*The best scenario for the family meeting would be . . .*

_____

_____

_____

_____

_____

*The worst scenario for the family meeting would be . . .*

_____

_____

_____

_____

_____

- Write out some of the challenges you may expect and how you will adjust to them. Play it out in your head.

_____

_____

_____

_____

_____

_____

_____

_____

_____

_____

## Roadblock #6: Consistency

Have you ever wondered why your child keeps asking for a cookie even though you have told him or her "no" several times over? The answer is your lack of consistency. Your child believes that it's well worth the gamble to keep asking because you've taught them that you will give in sooner or later. The odds are in their favor. Have you caught yourself doing this even as an adult?

Now, you will be setting up rules or guidelines as a family. Together you will agree upon an action step and its rewards and consequences. This takes the pressure off of you and permits you to act according to the guidelines decided upon. No knee-jerk reactions or randomly handing out rules and consequences. As a bonus, your family will have less ammunition to use in an argument.

I have the privilege of having two of my grandchildren spend a fair amount of time with me since their parents both work. Luke is eleven, and Sarah is nine. They are constantly fighting over screen time. Who's turn it is to choose a channel, a game, a device, or whatever. The manipulation and lying, screaming, and often physical tantrums and abuse was making life miserable. I had to do something. So, I set up a reward system, one point per hour depending on their behavior. They like getting treats or a small prize, so they were all in. We set up these rules:

1. One hour on and one hour off screen time alternately throughout their stay.
2. Respecting each other and learning how to work through problems is a vital skill we apply throughout life. Any negative

interactions that result in arguing and
other negative behavior will keep them
from gaining a point.

Our first two days went great, and they earned
their first prize; a small toy. Day three was a struggle.
Manipulation and lying were a constant. After Luke
lost points on the word of his sister, hysteria ensued.
It wasn't fair, etc. Sarah finally asked, "What happens if I give my brother one of my points?" We
talked about how she had exaggerated her story that
got her brother in trouble. In the end, she not only
gave him one of her points but gained one for her
honesty and generosity. What made her happiest was
being allowed to add and subtract the marks on the
chalkboard herself. Success! But the fight for consistency is an everyday battle.

Why did this work? We set a timer giving the
three of us the "stop break" signal and reminding us
to think about what comes next. Realizing that they
would get their devices back every other hour took
away the fear of losing them completely. Every hour
they cooperated, I put a point up on the chalkboard,
thanking them for their efforts. It worked because I
was predictable, they understood the how and why
we were doing this, and, most importantly, I was consistent.

· · ·

## Workbook 9E: Track Your Consistency

- Pick one or two of your new action steps and track your consistency using the Action Step Trackers below. Find something simple like, "I will look people in the eye when they are speaking to me." Practicing and becoming aware of how consistent you are will make it easier later on.

### Week 1

| Action steps: | | | | |
|---|---|---|---|---|
| Sun | | | | |
| Mon | | | | |
| Tues | | | | |
| Weds | | | | |
| Thurs | | | | |
| Fri | | | | |
| Sat | | | | |

## Week 2

| Action steps: | | | | |
|---|---|---|---|---|
| Sun | | | | |
| Mon | | | | |
| Tues | | | | |
| Weds | | | | |
| Thurs | | | | |
| Fri | | | | |
| Sat | | | | |

- After 2 weeks, reflect on how well you did. Remember, you're still practicing, so don't be so hard on yourself.

_____

_____

_____

**UNIQUE TO YOU (Use these lines for extra notes or to strategize.)**

# 10  WHAT SHOULD YOUR FIRST FAMILY MEETING INCLUDE?

The cat's out of the bag, so now what? How you introduce this exciting new direction is up to you. You are the only one who knows how to best approach your family. You could make an announcement at the dinner table, or perhaps using more of an individual approach to begin with could be better, knowing you need to gather as a family sooner or later. Stay confident! You now have so many tools to help you maneuver through this.

Remember to look at the Confidence Heart at the start of each chapter. All the tools we've talked about fit together to remind you of all the things you've mastered and how smart and skilled you are at using them. It is there to remind and encourage you.

.   .   .

## Workbook 10A: Schedule Your Family Meeting

- Decide on a date, time, and place for your family meeting.

_____

_____

_____

_____

## You've Got This!

Here are a few things that you've mastered. Remember to use all the puzzle pieces/tools and knowledge you have at your disposal to see you through each minute of each day.

- Remaining calm and smiling gives your family a sense that you're in control. It offers them a sense of security.
- You are now aware of the tug-of-war between body and soul and those old programs or knee-jerk reactions that no longer serve you. You know that they can be reprogrammed or deleted.

- You know how to use out-of-the-box thinking.
- You are getting better and better at diffusing your triggers.
- You have established an atmosphere of trust with your family.
- Your self-control is an exceptional example.
- You've learned to celebrate all the small successes.
- You have learned to manage your expectations.

## Workbook 10B: Invite Your Family to the Meeting

- Decide how you are going to invite your family to your first family meeting. Write it below, then take action.

_____

_____

_____

_____

_____

_____

_____

_____

_____

_____

## Preparing for Your Family Meeting

Preparing for my family meeting was the part I stewed about the most. I realized there was no magic spell that would make my whole family come together and cooperate the way I'd hope. I believe the frustration lies in my expectation to maintain control over everyone else in the group—like that could ever happen. Family meetings develop unity. Together, you learn social skills and problem-solving. It's a time to reconnect and bond as a unique group as you learn to respect and accept each other for who you each are. Home should be a sanctuary from the world.

## Creating an Agenda

- Know what you're going to say. Practice, including your body language and relaxation techniques.

- Hopefully, you've already discussed this with your significant other so you can work as a team. If points of contention remain, please try to find a way to compromise and commit to following through as agreed.
- Smile and remain calm. Take a deep breath in, and a long, slow exhale while envisioning the life you want for your family. You are strong and determined and ready to act in your family's best interest.
- Expect some negative reactions. Your family needs time to absorb what you're telling them. Do not let their comments and body language deter you from moving on. You have the power, and they know it. A smile indicates you've got it together.
- Start with an explanation. "I know I have been acting really weird lately about how I've been using my tech. You probably think I'm crazy, or maybe you're even afraid I'll turn off the Wi-Fi or take away your phones and games—no wonder you're feeling uncomfortable and perhaps even threatened. Don't worry, that's not going to happen. However, I think we need to talk as a family about how we're

using our devices and how we could spend more time interacting in the real world. I wanted to ask you guys how you feel about this, so we can help one another find ways to balance our screen time."

- Explain your concern; keep it simple and not dramatic. The kids might add that part.
- Set your family meeting rules that maintain a safe space, so that each of you can speak freely.
- Make a family vision statement. Setting a long-term goal for your family needs to be decided upon together. Ask for suggestions. Smile, listen, and remain calm and in control. Be sure everyone has their ideas heard and try to incorporate them within your statement and family rules. Now, post your family vision statement where you can all see it often.
- Decide when your next family meeting will be to choose your first action step, rewards, and consequences. Please don't put it off, or you'll have a hard time getting your family together again. Plan on no more than two days, but preferably the next day.

If you feel control slipping, say to yourself, "I'm right on schedule. Everything is going as expected!" Even negative comments mean that you are openly discussing this issue together.

**Workbook 10C: Create Family Meeting Agenda**
It will be easier going into your first family meeting if you know what you want to say beforehand.

- Have an agenda in mind—write the outline below. Remember to include time at the beginning to discuss your family meeting rules, why you are making these changes, and reassure them. After that, be sure to include in your outline time to create your family's vision statement, action steps, rewards system, and consequences. Know that not everything may get discussed in one meeting, but that is ok. It is progress nonetheless. Write your ideas and the words and relaxing techniques you will use. Practice your words and techniques.

_____

_____

Family Meeting Rules

Before the meeting, you'll need to set up some simple family meeting rules. Don't panic, these rules are probably rules you have already set in place. Your goal is to build an environment of trust where every voice can be heard. Once these rules are in place, you should have a more controlled get-together and be able to accomplish what you set out to do. Keep it simple. Here are a few suggestions:

- The Golden Rule: Do unto others as you would have them do unto you. Remember respect and consideration.
- Every voice must be heard without judgment.
- Think and act outside the box. Try to see from each other's perspectives.
- Take turns.

## Workbook 10D: Establish Your Family Meeting Rules

- Write your list of rules for the family to follow during the family meeting. Make

sure they are addressed at the beginning
of the meeting.

_____

_____

_____

_____

_____

_____

_____

_____

_____

_____

_____

_____

_____

_____

_____

_____

Now, stand tall and call your beautiful family together.

And don't forget: It's time to reward yourself. You are doing great!


**UNIQUE TO YOU (Use these lines for extra notes or to strategize.)**

_____

_____

_____

_____

_____

_____

_____

_____

_____

_____

_____

_____

# 11  FINALLY, MEET AS A FAMILY

Now that you have called your family together and you have already explained what the family meeting rules are, it's time for the nitty gritty.

## Creating Your Family's Vision Statement or Final Goal

Most companies or organizations have a vision statement that directs each employee's focus toward the company's goal. It gives everyone the reason *why* they want to help achieve this goal, uniting and motivating each individual to act, so that together, they will attain it. Here are two examples:

- Nike - "Bring inspiration and innovation

to every athlete* in the world. *If you have a body, you are an athlete."

- McDonald's - "To be the best quick service restaurant experience. Being the best means providing outstanding quality, service, cleanliness and value, so that we make every customer smile in every restaurant."

Your family needs a clear "why" and "where" you're heading together. This will help answer some of their concerns such as, "Is it worth the struggle, pain, discomfort, and the changes it will take to get there?"

Each personality will need this question answered in their own voice.

The dominant "D" personality needs to be invested in this goal and direct how it will be achieved.

The inspiring "I" type person will be the one who finds incentives through games and reward systems. They will help balance the consequences you set up, but mostly, they will inspire all of you while having fun, and they will lighten the load. It is the inspiring type who will remember to praise and uplift while going through change.

Our "S" or sensitive children will be resistant at first because they are uncomfortable with change. However, once they can see the benefit and accept the changes, they will be fully committed and supportive of others.

The cautious "C" type will need time to process the new information and calculate the pros and cons. They are terrific gatekeepers and can keep track of points and rewards.

Be sure everyone has their ideas heard and try to incorporate them within your statement. Maintain a safe space so each of you can speak freely. (This should be a part of your family meeting rules.)

Your vision statement should:

- Be clear and concise.
- Be future-oriented—think about what you want your family to become as your children grow up and move forward on their own.
- State why this is so important to you.
- Create a goal that is challenging but attainable by describing how you can achieve it.

For example: "We stand united to create a world of hope, joy, and innumerable possibilities by seeing, hearing, supporting, and respecting each other through life's challenges, allowing each of us to build a happy and productive future of our own design."

**What**—"We stand united to create a world of hope, joy, and innumerable possibilities . . ."

**How**—". . . by seeing, hearing, supporting, and respecting each other through life's challenges, . . ."

**Why**—". . . allowing each of us to build a happy and productive future of our own design."

Once you've created your vision statement, confirm with a high five, or a "Go, family!"

## Workbook 11A: Create Your Family's Vision Statement

- Create a vision statement the entire family can agree upon; this should include broad statements about what your family will be like in the future once you have learned to balance screen time.

_____

_____

_____

_____

_____

_____

_____

Once you finish your vision statement, take a final vote and confirm with a high five, a "Go, Family!", or a simple announcement that all have accepted your family statement.

Write out your vision statement on a separate sheet of paper and have everyone sign it. Hang it up in your home where everyone can see it.

## Action Steps

It's time to create your first action steps as a family. Have some ideas in mind. You've had time to analyze this information from many angles. You may discuss and discover several action steps your family could take. I suggest you one that you pick one that you can manage and succeed at. Any progress, even just teaching awareness, is a success. Manage your expectations and create a safe space.

For example, let's say your action step is no phones at the dinner table. Discuss how eating together is often the only time your family spends quality time together. This is only possible if all the phones are turned off or on airplane mode. Phones can be placed in a basket or another room during this time. Practicing separating from our devices teaches us that we can let go of them knowing they will be available for use later.

. . .

## Workbook 11B: Create Your Family's First Action Step(s)

You may discuss and discover several action steps your family could take in relation to your new foundational belief and ultimate goal. I suggest you start with just one—one you can manage, control, and succeed at. Failure is in the eye of the beholder.

Here are some ideas of beginner action steps:

- No phones at the dinner table.
- No phones in the bathrooms.
- No phones on short drives or when you're driving.
- No phones when in the store. Become aware of your surroundings. You just might see a familiar face.

Here are some examples of next-level action steps that build on themselves:

- Charge your phones in the central area of the house.
- Stop any screen time one to two hours before going to bed to allow the body to secrete melatonin to encourage sleep.
- No phones in the bedroom overnight. This

is an excellent first step to no phones in the private areas of the home, which may be a part of your final goal. It is here where questionable activity takes place that your child doesn't want you to know about.

Now, write your answers to the following questions:

- What is your ultimate goal?

_____

_____

_____

_____

_____

_____

_____

- What is an action step that will get you closer to your ultimate goal?

_____

_____

_____

_____

_____

_____

_____

_____

_____

_____

You have to decide what your final rules will be and work toward that. If you have a young family, you'll be setting up boundaries early on. It's much harder to take away from what's already familiar. Be patient and go at a pace that works best for your family. Warning: It will be easy to back off, but you will lose ground as time passes and either have to start again or give up. The only thing that will keep you moving forward is the vision you have set for your beautiful family in the future. The decisions you make today will determine that future.

## Rewards and Alternate Activities

Now that you have some action steps in place, you need a little positive reinforcement to make it worth the trouble. Rewards are not bribes or payoffs but recognition for each member's efforts with the understanding that change is hard.

When I first introduced the one-hour on and one-hour off plan for screen time with my grandchildren, Luke and Sarah had a hard time figuring out what to do during the off time. Having a list of options will make this part much easier, and everyone can add their incredible ideas to the list. You can use these activities as an individual or family reward.

Different types of activities will require either money, time, or both. Discover various activities and place them in categories by value, money, time, or all three. If need be, you can separate activities for younger and older children. Your family will have great ideas to add to your list. Determine what activities are considered positive screen time, such as writing or creating art. If they're like me—once I'm lost in a project, I need someone to remind me to take a break and set limits.

Giving my grandchildren an extra reward for when they spend more time off than on screen is an extra incentive. We rarely have to use the hour-on-hour-off system anymore because they are self-motivated and have other options knowing they can come back to their devices and have plenty of time to use them.

Remember, these are rewards, not bribes. Never pay out until they earn it. I've been caught in the trap of promises that are never fulfilled when the reward was given before the action was completed. That generally is not how it works out in the world, so it's a good time to teach them this point now.

A reward should be equal to the effort. You can select individual rewards, but in this case, since your goal is to create family unity, it might be fun to have something you can all enjoy together as well. Decide on your budget and go from there. Dinner out, a hike, or one of your favorite family activities could be fun options. Decide on the reward specifics ahead of time, connecting it to your action steps. It's like knowing you will get paid so much per hour at work.

You have all done such a good job! Remember to:

- Praise your family!
- Smile!
- Build an environment of trust.
- Remember that confrontation is a sign your child is working their way through change.
- Emphasize the "why."
- Love and value your child unconditionally.
- Make sure everyone has a voice.
- Discuss possible options available that will scale down their screen time. Be sure

to introduce the heavy hitters like screen time is only allowed in the family spaces.

- Let your family decide what the first action step will be.
- Write the action step out, why this step, what you are already doing to make this step doable, and what you still need to do.
- Create a reward system that works best for your family.
- Decide on the consequences. It is crucial that everyone has had a say and agrees to these terms. Write it out and sign it.
- Discuss alternate /downtime or reward activities, adding new ideas as they come to you.
- Journal to reinforce your dreams/goals or even celebrate your successes.
- Plan—Do—Check and Adjust. Reassess the effectiveness of your overall plan every four to seven days if not more often.

## Workbook 11C: Rewards/Alternate Activities

In your family meeting, discuss what kind of fun rewards you could do as a family. Do you know their value? Did you pick some fun combined family activities you can all do together?

- Reflect below.

_____

_____

_____

_____

_____

_____

_____

_____

_____

_____

## Workbook 11D: Consequences

You made a list of possible consequences in chapter 7. Refer to that and help your family find simple consequences that are equal to the action. Stop and hear them out before reacting.

- Write down your new list of agreed upon consequences.

_____

_____

_____

_____

_____

_____

_____

_____

_____

_____

_____

_____

_____

_____

Congratulations! It's time to celebrate. Have some ice cream!

**UNIQUE TO YOU (Use these lines for extra notes or to strategize.)**

_____

_____

_____

_____

_____

_____

_____

_____

_____

_____

_____

_____

_____

_____

# 12  JOURNAL YOUR JOURNEY

With your first family meeting out of the way, now it's up to you to maintain consistency to the rules you have set for yourself and your family. Stay strong in your beliefs and remember your "why." Before you get too wrapped up in the future, focus on the present. Check in with yourself and how you are feeling at this point in your journey to balancing your family's screen time.

Can you imagine reading through these changes later and remembering how crazy this whole thing was? It is also a great place to discover how many times you overcame different challenges, and use those techniques again in the future.

**Workbook 12A: Reflect on Your First Family**

## Meeting

Can you imagine reading through these changes later and remembering how crazy this whole thing was? It is also a great place to discover how many times you overcame different challenges, and use those techniques again in the future.

Journal how your meeting went and how it fits into your expectations. You can also use these notes as a reference should there be any question as to what you decided. Answer the following questions:

- What happened during the meeting?

_____

_____

_____

_____

_____

_____

_____

_____

_____

- How did your meeting compare with your expectations?

_____

_____

_____

_____

_____

_____

_____

_____

_____

_____

_____

_____

_____

_____

- What will I do differently next time?

_____

_____

_____

_____

_____

_____

_____

_____

_____

_____

_____

_____

_____

_____

Time to Plan, Do, Check, and Adjust

Be sure to schedule your next family meeting. It is important that you stop and evaluate how things are going. Fine-tune your action steps, rewards, consequences, and if needed, your family rules. You're doing great! Keep it up. Now, it's just a matter of doing it all over again, except the next time around, it will be much easier. Plan which action step you're going to add, then let it play out. Get together to check out how things are going and adjust as needed. You're heading toward the life you dreamed about in your vision statement.

## Workbook 12B: Schedule Your Next Family Meeting

Decide when your next family meeting will be. Keep it within a couple of days so you don't lose your momentum. In this next meeting, you are going to choose your first actions steps, rewards, and consequences, which are discussed in the next chapter.

- Write down the date, time, and location of your next family meeting.

_____

_____

_____

_____

_____

## Workbook 12C: Plan, Do, Check, and Adjust

Even after your second family meeting, be consistent and remember to plan, do, check, and adjust at least every four to seven days. Fine-tune your action steps, rewards, consequences, and if needed, your family rules. If needed, get together and see what needs to be adjusted and try again.

- Record any changes you make here.

_____

_____

_____

_____

_____

_____

Congratulations! You've done it again, one baby step at a time. Don't forget to celebrate.

As you go through this process of meeting together, re-evaluating, and adding new actions, remember to plan-do-check and adjust to fine-tune your action steps, rewards, consequences, and if needed, your family rules. You're doing great! Keep it up.

The next chapters probably address some of the most concerning issues parents have to deal with—for sure, they can be the scariest. Once you're familiar with the information, be sure to include action steps relating to digital citizenship, including screen time etiquette, safety, and how your family values impact these.

**UNIQUE TO YOU (Use these lines for extra notes or to strategize.)**

_____

_____

_____

_____

_____

# 13 WORDS ARE LETHAL WEAPONS: CYBERBULLYING

"Sticks and stones will break my bones, but words will never hurt me."

Whoever first created this phrase probably didn't actually believe it was true but instead tried to use it as a shield to deflect the pain words can produce. The rice experiment from Chapter 6 proved that words have energy. As the waveforms of words move from one person to another, they are absorbed, creating a chemical reaction, either positive or negative. Words are the weapons cyberbullies use to destroy another's soul to fill in their own negative spaces.

Sadly, we may all catch ourselves sending harmful and sometimes hurtful messages to someone else, even though we know the pain it causes. It's time to become more aware of our words. Should we slip, quickly apologize and make up for the pain we just inflicted.

Cyberbullies understand the power of words. They know and often strategize how they can have the most devastating effects on their victims, not only with words but with videos, provoking their victims to lose their tempers and act rashly. Hiding behind the screen makes these bullies feel even more empowered because no one is around to judge them, and there's no immediate accountability. They don't have to see the pain in their victim's eyes. Sadly, many of these bullies torture their victims just for the fun of it. But not every cyberbully is bent on destruction; many are children trying to fit in, making jokes, and not seeing the consequences of their actions.

## What Is Cyberbullying?

"Willful harm inflicted through the use of computers, cell phones, and other electronic devices . . . cyberbullying is when someone repeatedly makes fun of another person online or repeatedly picks on another person through email or text message or when someone posts something online about another person that they don't like. While the action of uploading a picture/post is a one-time behavior, others can view it or otherwise refer to it repeatedly, thereby resulting in recurring humiliation and shame to the target. One person might see it, or millions of people might see it."[1]

As a parent and grandparent, I am often unable to react to this threat in a rational manner. It brings on fear of a problem I can't prevent or one that I could be unaware of. What do I do once I know my grandchildren's innocent souls have been scared? I may downplay an incident and lose the trust these children have put in me. We're the adults—we're supposed to protect them. To better understand this threat, it's time to understand it and how we can help. .

## The 10 Types of Cyberbullying (*Kid Safety* by Kaspersky)

1. Exclusion: deliberately leaving someone out.
2. Harassment: intentional and constant messages that are abusive and threatening.
3. Outing: to intentionally embarrass or humiliate a child or group by posting embarrassing information without consent, including private information.
4. Cyberstalking: bullying that includes threats of physical harm, which includes predatory actions by adults.
5. Fraping: posting on someone else's

accounts and impersonating them to get them in trouble.

6. Fake Profiles: to cover up their cyberbullying activity

7. Dissing: posting cruel information to damage a friendship or reputation.

8. Trickery: gaining a child's trust by befriending them to gain sensitive information they plan to exploit.

9. Trolling: deliberately provoking a response to make their victim look bad.

10. Catfishing: stealing a child's online identity, photos, and building social networking profiles for deceptive purposes.

Knowing this may make you uncomfortable but ignoring it could end up being a fatal mistake.

Spend some time talking about cyberbullying in a family meeting. Now that you're aware, what can you and your children do about it? (This is a possible action step opportunity.)

**Workbook 13A: Identify Types of Cyberbullying**

- Below, name three types of cyberbullying you want to discuss with your children.

_____

_____

_____

_____

_____

_____

_____

The Cyberbullying Research Center provides up-to-date information about all phases of cyberbullying including the causes, and consequences of how cyberbullying affects our adolescents. This and other resources are available to you. Below is some of the information they have collected.

Depending on age, the number of youth who experience cyberbullying ranges from 10-40 percent.[2] This includes incidents of repeatedly making fun of or picking on another person.

In 2019, a group of 5,000 middle and high school students reported these facts about cyberbullying:[3]

- 36.5% had been bullied in their lifetime
- 17.4% had been bullied in the last thirty days
- 14% admitted to cyberbullying in their lifetime

- 14.9% had witnessed cyberbullying
- 94% reported that bullying had negatively impacted their life
- 33% reported that bullying had affected their friendships
- 13% reported that bullying had affected their physical health
- 6.5% reported that bullying had affected their schoolwork
- 63% said they were willing to step in to defend and support others being bullied

## Workbook 13B: Have Your Child/Children Self-Reflect

- Allow your children to discover times they may have been guilty of cyberbullying. Record their response.

_____

_____

_____

_____

_____

- Also ask your child if they have been a victim of cyberbullying. Record their response.

_____

_____

_____

_____

_____

_____

_____

_____

_____

_____

_____

_____

_____

_____

When our children's safety is threatened, they are unable to move on and engage in growing activities such as education. Maslow's Hierarchy of Needs states that once safety becomes our focus, we cannot move forward and focus on belonging and friendship, let alone doing schoolwork.

The constant influx of negativity bores into your child's mind, and they no longer believe that they have any self-worth, and that there's no way to regain it. It is like being invisible, and like the rice that was ignored in our experiment, it shrivels, becomes dark and moldy, and dries up. Depression and anxiety overtake them, and for many, the only way out is suicide. Dramatic, yes, but not for the families that have lost their child to the inability to cope.

It's time to engage and accept that cyberbullying is a severe problem that must be dealt with.

## Cyberbullying is Prosecutable

Be aware that all posts are permanent. The government can find past posts, even those that have been deleted, and hold them against you years later. You now have a "record," and it will come up in all your future background checks throughout the rest of your life.

. . .

## Workbook 13C: Watch the Cyberbullying Video for Schools

Watch the video, "Cyberbullying Video for Schools,"[4] and discuss it with your family.

- What were their thoughts? What action step(s) could you set in place to prevent cyberbullying situations?

_____

_____

_____

_____

_____

_____

_____

_____

_____

_____

_____

_____

_____

## Cyberbullying Apps Parents Should Know About

You may be surprised at which companies are listed in an online article by *Securly*.[5] None of them support cyberbullying in any way, but are a part of social media all of us have access too.

YOLO links to Snapchat; it is an anonymous app that encourages rumor-spreading and hate speech. It is reported that both Apple and Google have dropped them.

Instagram gives bullies an easy way to criticize posts through comments and messaging anonymously.

*Ditch the Label* reported that more than one in five 12-to-20-year-olds experience bullying, specifically on Instagram.[6]

Facebook's platform keeps expanding as well as the many ways cyberbullies can take advantage of your child; derogatory comments or threats, public profiles, pages, posts of sensitive and embarrassing images. They can create pages or groups with the intent of tormenting their victims.

On Snapchat, inappropriate content is still posted, saved, and shared privately among friends. Snapchat has since upped its efforts to try to stop users from abusing the app. Read more about what features are available to help pinpoint digital bullying at the source on *Webwise*.[7]

YouTube has been facing a lot of backlash over what some call a "selectively enforced harassment policy." Because of this, people started a movement against cyberbullying. Watch the powerful video that started the #CreateNoHate campaign.[8]

Twitter continues to fight cyberbullies who abuse the platform with fake accounts. While it continues to be an issue, Twitter has spent the last two years implementing ways for users to report and take action against threats, hate speech, impersonation, and harassment.

For more information on cyberbullying and how to tackle it, check out the following informational articles:

- 7 Tips on Keeping Your Child Safe Online[9]
- 11 Facts About Cyberbullying[10]

If you feel you or your children are being bullied online, call the cyberbullying hotline number at 1-800-273-8255 for cyberbullying help.

**Workbook 13D: Your Child's Social Media Access**

- Which social media site(s) does your child access?

_____

_____

_____

_____

_____

_____

- Are those sites acceptable to you? Why or why not?

_____

_____

_____

_____

_____

_____

_____

- Set social media rules and teach your children why they are necessary. Examples include setting a time limit for how long they are allowed to be on social media every day/week or setting a rule that they can only use social media when an adult is present. You can also set restrictions related to who they follow. Record your rules/restrictions below.

_____

_____

_____

_____

_____

_____

_____

_____

_____

_____

_____

_____

## Roadblocks That Keep Us from Addressing This Issue

Parents might:

- Disregard it or think there are more serious problems.
- Lack the knowledge and time to track their child's online activity.
- Believe the schools should be teaching online precautions.

Educators might:

- Teach online safety but are unsure how to intervene or fear the after-effects it will have.

Law enforcement:

- HIB law—Harassment, Intimidation and Bullying—defines specific actions law enforcement can take. As with all our laws the purpose is to protect the innocent, sometimes in this process the bad guy gets away. They must protect the rights of the victim and the offender.

We need to:

- Understand that the more time our child spends online, the greater the risk of victimization is.
- Know how others are connecting with our children. Be aware of and be able to monitor your child's online activity.
- Teach our children how to develop resilience and grow through the more minor struggles, giving them the capabilities to stand firm through life's challenges.
- Let our children know we are there for them by building an environment of trust.
- Send the message that there are consequences attached to cyberbullying.
- Allow educators to intervene without fear of parental retaliation.
- Be aware of the laws and how to use them.
- Work together as a community to protect our children.

**UNIQUE TO YOU (Use these lines for extra notes or to strategize.)**

# 14 THE POWER WITHIN YOUR HOME

You have come so far. You've accepted a new foundational belief that balancing screen time is worth fighting for and are taking steps to protect your family. The power in our homes is us—it's our determination and love that drives us forward. Understanding how to communicate with our children and educating both them and ourselves is vital. Without this crucial information, we cannot protect them and our children will continue to be unaware and unable to protect themselves. We need to know how and where these threats are coming from, and how they are connecting with our children in order to continue to fight this fight.

## Creating Trust Through Open Discussion

Building an environment of trust is integral to creating open communication. Talking about your child's device use without judgment and creating trust that you won't take their phone away except in extreme circumstances allows you to discuss your concerns openly and find a solution together. In the end, you are only in control of your own actions, and your child is free to choose and experience the consequences.

Stand strong to the consequences list you have created as a family. Teach them how to problem-solve and discover that they are stronger than they think. Allowing them to fall so they can learn how to get back up builds resilience, keeping them from crumbling at the first sign of a threat. Part of that is taking on the responsibility of their own actions, starting with the responsibility of being a digital citizen.

## Digital Citizenship

Being a part of a digital society holds the same responsibilities and risks as living in the physical world. Courtesy and bullying are part of being human, however, in the digital world we often seem to forget that because we are not directly interacting with each other. Just because you can't see the other person's response doesn't mean it didn't happen, good or bad. We need to show the same respect whether we are communicating online or in person.

## Digital Safety

We have the ability to protect our families by using these simple steps:

- Be aware of and take measures against potential risk.
- Never share any personal information to prevent misuse that threatens your safety.
- Parental involvement influences how a teen behaves responsibly and appropriately.

## Digital Etiquette

Digital Etiquette should be self-explanatory, but when the offender is behind the screen, they feel less vulnerable and freer to act without thought of the consequences.

- Use the same social guidelines you would use if you were interacting face-to-face.
- Be courteous when using devices around

other people or in social settings. Put your phone down to talk to or listen to someone. Be respectful in groups, ceremonies, or other formal settings, and keep your phone in your pocket out of respect.

- Report cyberbullying to protect your friends; consequences decrease cyberbullying.

A great resource is StopBullying.gov. [1]

## Workbook 14A: Actions Steps Toward Digital Citizenship

Now that you're aware of digital citizenship, safety, etiquette, and reporting, what can you and your children do about it? Reflect.

- What are your action steps toward improving your and your children's digital citizenship?

_____

_____

_____

_____

_____

_____

_____

_____

_____

_____

_____

_____

- What are your action steps toward protecting your children's digital safety?

_____

_____

_____

_____

_____

_____

_____

_____

_____

_____

_____

_____

_____

_____

_____

- What are your action steps for your children to better understand digital etiquette and reporting?

_____

_____

_____

_____

_____

_____

_____

_____

_____

_____

_____

_____

_____

_____

## Think Before You Post

Teenagers, like children, are impulsive and unable to stop and think before acting. A fourteen-year-old girl wanted to stop the pain so many of her peers felt due to cyberbullying. She created the Rethink app.[2] Each time a threatening or cruel text is written, the app sends an alert asking them if they truly want to send it. This simple stop-break allows the child to stop and think before clicking send.

·  ·  ·

## Workbook 14B: Install the Rethink App

The Rethink app is free and a great tool to help get people to stop and think before sending a hurtful message. You can watch an overview on how to use it on YouTube.[3] Test it out; did it work? Be careful not to send your test text out.

- Do you think this app could be a good reminder after you've written a scathing text while you were still wrapped in emotion? Reflect.

_____

_____

_____

_____

_____

_____

_____

_____

_____

## Stranger Danger

We used to warn our children about "stranger danger" when going out into the world. Stranger danger now comes into our homes or wherever we carry our devices. It's time to have an open discussion with our children. Continue to build an environment of trust. Sixty-two percent of students polled in a recent study by Win Win Parenting said they wouldn't tell their parents if they were being bullied online.[4] What are they afraid of? Judgment, embarrassment, the inability to be smart enough to handle their phone, or the fear of losing their phone privileges, their lifeline to their world.

Brent Scarpo, a well-known intuitive life coach, believes that our children are so in tune with the load we as parents already carry that adding their problems of bullying would be a further burden.[5] Whatever the reason, we need to find a way to open communication with our children. We often don't realize how we talk about our lives as adults, which is then overheard and processed by our children, whether we intended for them to hear it or not.

## Defenses Against Cyberbullying

Whether your child is currently dealing with cyberbullying or not, they should all know the following ways to defend against it (*WellCast*, Cyberbullying protection guide[6]):

- Do not respond or retaliate . That's what the bully needs and wants. They thrive on your reaction and the power they have to elicit it. It is the only thing that maintains their own self-worth. It makes them feel powerful.
- Block the bully if possible.
- Be brave and trust your parents or responsible adults—that may include a hotline number. Don't be afraid of their judgment; even if they slip up in the end, they want to be involved in keeping you safe. Nobody expects a child or anyone else to endure this on their own.
- Make it impossible for them to find you.
- Set up your messaging system so that only those on your buddy list can get through.
- Block individual screen names or try going invisible when necessary.
- Screen all incoming phone calls and text messages.
- Suspend your social media pages and disappear from the internet.
- Save the evidence and tell someone; only then will the bully understand that

there are consequences to his or her actions.

## Workbook 14C: Choose Your Defensive Steps

- Record which of the above defensive steps you have set in place. Did you or your child come up with others? Write them down.

_____

_____

_____

_____

_____

_____

_____

_____

_____

_____

_____

## Workbook 14D: Set Protective Limits

- Go through the list below and check off protective limits you will use with your family. Set protective limits that fit your family best.

_____ Trust your parents or responsible adult; that may include a hotline number.

_____ Privacy Controls—set to private.

_____ Set up your messaging system so that only those on your buddy list can get through.

_____ Block individual screen names or try going invisible when necessary.

_____ Screen all incoming phone calls and text messages.

_____ Suspend your social media pages and disappear from the internet.

_____ Save the evidence and tell someone; only then will the bully understand that there are consequences to his actions.

## Privacy Controls

Together with your children, sit down and check the profile settings of your social media accounts to ensure they are set to private. This can stop strangers from contacting and viewing your posts. Give your child the power to protect themselves and their friends. There is a video that will guide you through how to do this.[7]

## Set Guidelines

Fortunately, we have already discussed possible guidelines to balance and protect your family. Sit down and discuss if there are any other suggestions you or your children have that may seem more reasonable now that you understand the threat your devices can bring into your home. Build age and stage appropriate limits into one of your action steps that will help create the new habit.

- All devices are to be charged in the central area of the house.
- Phones should not be used in the private areas of your home—bedrooms, bathrooms etc. It is usually here that you hide what you are doing because you already feel like something is not right.

- No phones in the bedrooms overnight. Whether what they are watching is harmful or not, the temptation of the phone is overpowering and will disrupt your child's sleep. It also disrupts brain function since their bio-computer is unable to shut down and reboot.
- Use parental controls. You control the Wi-Fi, electricity, and the devices in your homes. There are videos on how to set up parental controls on YouTube[8] and on an iPad or iPhone.[9]

## Workbook 14E: Set Guidelines

Work together with your children to set protective guidelines.

- Which controls did you set up?

_____

_____

_____

_____

_____

_____

_____

_____

_____

_____

_____

_____

**UNIQUE TO YOU (Use these lines for extra notes or to strategize.)**

_____

_____

_____

_____

_____

_____

_____

_____

# 15  YOU'RE NOT ALONE

The greatest advantage any "bully" has is making us feel like we're alone. There are so many resources available to us from people fighting for our children. Programs like Bark or Screentime Labs offer us services to help protect our children. They also have support systems in place to walk you through any of your concerns.

## Spying on Your Kids or Monitoring Possible Threats

It has been suggested that we monitor our children's phone activity, looking for any signs that may raise a red flag. In our world where we have been given rights and freedoms, we may bock at this idea.

Does teaching your child to be careful around fire

restrict their freedom? You understand that fire burns and causes a great deal of pain and harm. You are forewarning them so they will not get burned. You now know that your child's devices are a gateway to bullies and predators and the more time they spend online, the more likely they will be found and hurt. You can choose to respect your child's privacy and remain oblivious and unaware of their need for help, or you can help them by sorting through the infinite amount of information that is being thrust upon them and help them become aware and learn to protect themselves.

## Workbook 15A: Investigate Monitoring Systems

Investigate monitoring systems that are able to help you monitor your children's online activity. The two monitoring services I like that have made it easier and less invasive are Bark and Screentime.

These programs look for tell-tale signs that may indicate a threat and alert you to investigate further. They can help you determine when your children can access the internet on their devices and which sites they can visit. They also have support systems in place to walk you through any of your concerns. Collect the information you need to make a decision about which system would best work for you.

- Record your findings.

_____

_____

_____

_____

_____

_____

_____

_____

_____

_____

_____

_____

_____

## Be the Example!

"Do as I say and not as I do" does not work. Children mirror your actions and those of others. Please don't learn this lesson the hard way. Any of these action steps you set up with your children are also your action steps. Just because you're an adult doesn't mean you are not at risk. Cyberbullies and predators don't care as long as they get the results they want. They will seek out the young and vulnerable because they are easy targets. Besides, it's all for naught if you don't follow your own rules, it gives your children permission to do the same.

## Workbook 15B: Set Rules for Yourself

- Create a new foundational belief system relating to being the example to your children. Whether you want it or not, they will mirror what you do. Ask yourself, "Will my example create the result I was hoping for?"

_____

_____

_____

_____

_____

_____

_____

_____

_____

_____

_____

_____

## School Safety

As parents, we have placed a great deal of responsibility on our school system to help raise our children. We expect schools to educate them on facts and social skills, responsibility, and accountability for their actions, social safety, and appropriate interaction. However, teachers can't grade a child in compliance with how their students use their devices or implement the belief systems each student grew up with. If they had that kind of control, we wouldn't need this book.

Teachers are honored to serve your children but need your support. Raising our children to become resilient, responsible adults takes a team effort. Think about how frustrating it is when your significant other says one thing when you expected another. This is the same relationship parents have with teachers. You can't teach responsibility without consequences, and teachers' hands are often tied, and their jobs are threatened by unreasonable expectations.

According to the *Cyberbullying Research Center*[1], schools should:

- Provide a safe environment within the school.
- Promote awareness through classroom instruction and assemblies about all forms of bullying and the risk of school and legal penalties.
- Make the students aware of the emotional, psychological, reputational, and physical harm cyberbullying can cause.
- Let students know they have a responsibility to report cyberbullying and create open lines of communication by knowing students' names, showing compassion and empathy beyond academics, creating an atmosphere of trust.

- Develop community relationships with businesses, non-profits, law enforcement, youth professionals, and parents to reinforce mutual respect and safety. It takes a village to defeat the threat cyberbullying has created.
- Set up anonymous reporting through a school web page, confidential phone number for text or voice. Encourage swift and appropriate reporting. Act quickly to the evidence given. Students should know that adults at school have their backs, that they genuinely care for, and want to help and protect them.
- Student empowerment enlists the students' passion for helping and solving problems as a powerful tool. Peers that promote positive attitudes, beliefs, and behavior have a powerful effect on the school environment.
- Promote a positive atmosphere within the school that recognizes all the positive actions and kindness that is the norm in schools.

## Workbook 15C: Support Your Children's Schools

Find a way to support your children's schools by getting involved.

- Know your resources: which teacher, administrator, or others can you report to? Write them down here.

_____

_____

_____

_____

_____

_____

_____

- What is the hotline number that you would call within your school?

_____

_____

- Does the school have any other available program that the school suggests to assist in protecting your children's digital safety?

_____

_____

_____

_____

_____

_____

_____

## Team-Up

More and more our children are finding their voices by standing together against the victimization of their fellow students. This gives them the combined strength and confidence to stand for what's right. This includes the confidential routes for reporting abuses within the schools. The more data that is collected about how much, what kind, and how harmful activity affects others, the more ammunition or proof our administrators have to get the help they need to fight this crisis. Our children count on us to act on this information.

Never stop learning and researching. Knowledge and programs like Rethink and Bark are vital tools when fighting cyberbullies and predators to protect our children. Find a parent support group where you can discuss your concerns and support each other.

"Reconnecting with our Families that have been lost behind their screens" is the name of the Facebook group I have created focused on supporting each other. Join us!

## Law Enforcement

Sadly, bullying has become so prominent that a law had to be written to help protect this country's citizens and provide a consequence for offenders.

HIB Law makes bullying of any kind prosecutable. Here is the chain of command this law flows through[2]:

- The incident is reported to the principal.
- The principal must report all incidents to the anti-bullying specialist.
- The principal is to contact both the offender and the victim's parents and offer support options.
- The school's anti-bullying specialist submits their report to the chief school administrator.
- The chief school administrator can report the results of the investigation to both sets of parents. He also sends the information to the Board of Education.
- The Board of Education submits a written

decision based on the chief school administrator's report.

- The Board of Education reports the decision to the parents.
- Parents can request a hearing in front of the Board of Education. The hearing must be within ten days of the request.
- Should this still be unsatisfactory, parents can contact the County Office of Education.

## Workbook 15D: Know the Laws Against Cyber-bullying

Law enforcement is there to protect you, but in doing so, they also have to monitor and control those who may harm you, often making them the "bad guys." Without them, we would be living in great chaos as the bullies take over control.

- What is the name of the law that addresses cyberbullying, and what does it enforce?

_____

_____

_____

_____

_____

_____

_____

- Take the time to talk to your children about this important subject. Later on, review how your discussion went and how you can reinforce it again.

_____

_____

_____

_____

_____

_____

_____

_____

_____

_____

# UNIQUE TO YOU (Use these lines for extra notes or to strategize.)

_____

_____

_____

_____

_____

_____

_____

_____

_____

_____

_____

_____

_____

_____

# 16 THE ULTIMATE CYBERBULLY: THE PREDATOR

A parent's greatest fear is that their child might be taken, hurt, or killed. The stories that run through our minds of what could be happening to them are terrifying. We can pretend it will never happen to our family, or we can take actions that will decrease those chances.

Sadly, a mother lost her young daughter to a cyber predator. She shared her story on YouTube. It's called "Oblivious." (See below in the workbook activity.) This story video shows you the steps the predator took and how her daughter responded. It is heart-breaking, but she shared her story to help keep your children safe, whether they're a girl or a boy.

Our teens are oblivious. Believing it only happens to someone else creates a barrier where the possibility is non-existent, so they live their lives moment by moment, not realizing the risks they are putting themselves in.

## Workbook 16A: Watch and Discuss with Your Children

Take the time to talk to your children. Watch the You-Tube video "Oblivious" together.[1] Answer the questions below.

- What were some of the steps the predator used?

_____

_____

_____

_____

_____

_____

_____

- What led up to this girl getting kidnapped? What could you and your family do to keep any of you from becoming the victim?

_____

_____

_____

_____

_____

_____

_____

_____

_____

_____

## Exposing Oneself

Our children's beliefs often draw in the predators. Posting inappropriate images has become acceptable. I once heard a young girl say, "What's the problem? It's how our generation does it. It's not a big deal." These activities draw the perpetrator in on our children who don't understand the horrible consequences that could follow.

The information our children are being taught related to sexuality is explicit and easily attainable. In their quest to be accepted, they will use any tool they can. Guidelines related to sexuality are set in the home. What they are allowed to watch or hear, they are allowed to do. Only you, as parents, can determine the boundaries you want to set. Understanding consequences and following through is vital. Not until your child has been given the information they need can they choose how they act. Remember they still lack the control of an adult and will often act before thinking it through.

## Workbook 16B: Precautions

Time to let go of the "it will never happen to me" mindset or any other belief that puts your child at risk, and replace it with a new foundational belief that will allow you to take the precautions needed to teach and protect your child from predators.

- What is your new foundational belief?

_____

_____

_____

_____

_____

## Sexting

This is a subject parents might feel uncomfortable talking to their children about. However, the attitude towards sex has become so open and free. Our children are being constantly bombarded with insinuations and often direct information and visuals that it becomes too enticing to avoid, or for many, it is thrust upon them. With this attitude being shared so freely, we need to address it in some manner with our children. Sexting may be, as one girl put it, "what our generation does," but it has consequences they don't believe would ever happen to them.

Sexting is making sexual images and posting them online. Teens often consider this fun and consensual, part of relationship building, self-confidence, and exploring their own sexuality. Some teens send these images to people they have never met, but others try to reduce the risk by sending directly to people they trust.

Talk to your teen. Creating that trusting environment will open up communication as your teen is exposed to sexting. Ask questions. Share your concerns and why you support or don't support this activity. Remember, posts are permanent and create a digital footprint that stays in the public domain forever. Once you've sent the image, you lose control of where it goes next.

Explain the legal consequences; remember, anything you do online is the same as doing it in public. This act must be consensual, including those you share this with, and those who will be offended by it.

Talk about respectful relationships and trust and be sure your child knows he or she has the right to say "no." Remind your teens about consequences like embarrassment, guilt and shame, and feeling uncomfortable.

There are many valuable resources about sexting like *KidsHelpLine*[2] and RaisingChildren.net.au.[3]


## Workbook 16C: Protect Against Sexting

I know this is an uncomfortable subject, but it's one that needs to be addressed. Becoming aware may be your child's only self-defense.

- List and describe three actions you can take on your children's behalf to protect against sexting.

_____

_____

_____

_____

_____

_____

_____

_____

_____

_____

_____

## Facts Every Parent Should Know and Share About Predators

A predator is only one step away from cyberbullying. The problem is that we don't believe it could happen to us, while the truth is if you or your child are on-line, you are opening yourself up to being bullied just as easily as your computer can be hacked. Any predator can find and trick you. They know what to say and how to play with your child. They understand that being accepted and valued is vital to a child/teen's existence, and they will use that against them. They understand that they are both innocent and inexperienced, but coming into themselves and trying to find their independence. Predators pretend to free them from the confines of your family by imprisoning them in their twisted and cruel world.

Like the young girl in "Oblivious,"[4] your child

can follow the predator's manipulations and fall into his or her trap. It's way too easy. If we can educate and convince our children that there is an actual threat and that we as parents can be trusted, we have a greater chance at keeping our children safe.

According to the *Puresight*[5]:

- Approximately 95% of children between ages 12 and 17 can access the internet.
- 1 in 5 say they have received unwanted sexual solicitations.
- 30% of the victims are boys.
- Predators are between ages 18 and 55 and target children between ages 11 and 15.
- 100% of the victims go willingly.
- 75% percent of children share personal information online.
- 33% of teens have friended people online they have never met in person.

## Grooming—How the Spider Catches Its Prey

Eric Marlowe Garrison defines grooming as "the slow, methodical, and intentional process of manipulating a person to a point where they can be victimized."[6] After the perpetrators find their targets, they then gain trust and move in from there.

Anyone can be a victim. Perpetrators target the

vulnerable, the young, inexperienced children, and the insecure and lonely by building trust. This kind of person never considers that they are being targeted and trusts freely.

It often starts with friendship. During this time, groomers get to know their victim. They usually follow the victim's posts and collect information about them and their contacts. This is one reason everyone—including our teens or even young adults—watch what they're posting. They may believe it would never happen to them or that they'd know it was happening. The reality is that's what all the other victims thought as well.

Groomers will use information, opinions, name dropping, mutual acquaintances, and social media platforms to collect the intel they need to use against their victims.

Perpetrators use favors and promises to build trust. As victims let down their guard and begin to see the perp as a friend, mentor, benefactor, or sexual interest, they will do a favor for them, so that the victims begins to feel indebted to them. The groomer will also find a way to explain why his or her act should remain a secret.

Over time, the groomer will actively try to separate the victim from anyone who would be protective, such as family and friends. They flatter their victims, making them believe they are someone special to them. They begin to insert themselves into the victim's everyday life.

Once a physical relationship is established, secrecy increases as well as shame and threats, controlling the relationship. The more they keep their victim cut off from other people, the more power they have.

Grooming can be difficult to distinguish from romance. One of the signs that may help you distinguish between the two is when you begin to feel like a victim. Another is the insistence to meet. Groomers have invested a lot and can see the progress they are making. This revs them up. Their desire to see you exceeds the excitement of someone in a new relationship. It turns into guilting and threatening. Grooming is not a mutual relationship. The victim is to be used and played with like a toy.

Signs to watch out for if you believe someone is being victimized may include:

- Alcohol and drug use
- Nightmares
- Change in diet and exercise
- Insomnia
- Eating disorders
- Anxiety
- Withdrawal
- Bedwetting (in kids)
- Risk-taking

- Acting inappropriately sexual for their age
- Self-harm or suicidal tendencies

A consenting relationship is one that flows freely between partners showing compassion and care. In a negative, grooming type of relationship, it becomes one-sided and often abusive. You can learn more about online predators at commonsensemedia.org.[7]

## Workbook 16D: Predator Warning Signs

- List three of the steps a predator/groomer would use to draw his/her victim in.

_____

_____

_____

_____

_____

_____

_____

_____

_____

- What would be a victim's first indicator that something is wrong?

_____

_____

_____

_____

_____

_____

_____

- Are all groomers intentional or aware of what they are doing? Why or why not?

_____

_____

_____

_____

_____

_____

_____

## Victims Can Get Free

There is hope. Once a victim has accepted their relationship as unhealthy, they are able to act. It seems like that would be an obvious decision, but it's not that easy. In a controlling or abusive relationship, there is a great deal of fear—fear of how their abuser will react, fear of the unknown. Where will I go? What can I do? How can I protect myself and others?

*Allure Magazine*[8] shares this information:

- Find a third party—someone who doesn't know the groomer, preferably a professional, or call the National Domestic Violence Hotline at (800-799-7233) or Victim Connect Resource Center (855-484-2846) These resources will connect you to the help you need confidentially.

Family and friends can help but tread lightly. Do not try to intervene, especially if the victim feels they don't need help. Be their friend, build trust and listen. Express your concerns and the reasons why. If an abuser senses a threat to their control, they may become even more abusive.

"Do not blame the victim. Believe them. Support them. Get help for them and you." -Marlow Garrison

. . .

## Workbook 16E: Free the Victim

- How can victims free themselves from a predator/groomer? How can a victim find his or her way out?

_____

_____

_____

_____

_____

_____

_____

_____

_____

_____

What's In Your Control Now?

It is your job to protect your child the best you can. A parent who lost their child to a predator would give anything to fight with that child again about phone restrictions, bullying, and predators.

You can do this by:

- Creating a foundational belief relating to keeping your children safe.
- Creating and acting on action steps needed to secure their safety.
- Following the steps you've learned to help assure compliance.
- Believing it could happen to you.

Your responsibility is to love unconditionally and teach and guide your children, accepting that they are in control of themselves no matter the consequences.

Love them unconditionally and act as best you can in their best interest. Talk to your higher power. He will give you the strength, comfort, and guidance to see you through this. He knows your pain and the pain your child is feeling.


## Workbook 16F: Teach to Avoid Predatory Relationships

Take control! Create a foundational belief and act on action steps that will keep your children safe and decrease the chances of your child being caught in this type of a relationship.

- Create a foundational belief with your children about avoiding predatory relationships.

_____

_____

_____

_____

_____

_____

- What are the action steps you will take to align with your new foundational belief?

_____

_____

_____

_____

_____

_____

_____

_____

_____

_____

_____

_____

**UNIQUE TO YOU (Use these lines for extra notes
or to strategize.)**

_____

_____

_____

_____

_____

_____

_____

_____

_____

# EPILOGUE

Congratulations! Here you are at the end of the book, but it's not the end of your story. No matter how far you got or how you feel right now, you are a success. Look how much you've learned and experienced. Don't let your expectations tear you down. This is a big undertaking to involve your entire family. If you believe that, in the end, balancing your screen time will make a difference, then don't give up the fight. Kids don't always understand in the moment, but in time, they will see the difference it makes. Stand strong. It's what your children expect of you even if they don't act like it. They need to know that as their parents, you are there for them and they don't have to maneuver this crazy world on their own.

Continue to add more screen time action steps

and repeat the process over again until you have achieved the balance you desire.

This parenting technique is not just for screen time. You can create new foundational beliefs for anything including amazing trips or other family or personal challenges. You did this together one way or another, and that's an achievement in itself. Keep up the good fight. Like He-Man, stand tall, raise your arm to the sky and proclaim, "I HAVE THE POWER!"

Please share your experience and how your family has worked together by emailing me at balancingscreentime@gmail.com, or share your thoughts in a testimonial on Amazon so others can enjoy this experience as well.

Find me at:

balancingscreentime.com

"Reconnecting with our Families that have been lost behind their screens" on Facebook.

# NOTES

## Introduction

1. Thomas Kersting. *Disconnected: How to Protect Your Kids from the Harmful Effects of Device Dependency.* Baker Books, 2020.
2. Tedx Talks. (2018, March 9). *iGen: The Smartphone Generation | Jean Twenge | TEDxLangunaBlancaSchool* [Video]. YouTube. https://www.youtube.com/watch?v=UA8kZ-ZS_bzc&list=RDCMUCsT0YIqwnpJCM-mx7-gSA4Q&index=1.

## 1. Steve Jobs and Bill Gates Raise Their Children Tech-Free

1. *Business Insider,* Allana Akhtar, & Marguerite Ward (2020, May 15). Bill Gates and Steve Jobs raised their kids with limited tech — and it should have been a red flag about our own smartphone use. https://www.businessinsider.com/screen-time-limits-bill-gates-steve-jobs-red-flag-2017-10
2. Moghul B. (2018, August 3). Steve Jobs Kids Don't Use Electronic Devices - Ted Talk [Video]. YouTube. https://www.youtube.com/watch?v=qww1NNf2aeY
3. Bilton, Nick. "Steve Jobs was a low-tech parent." The Sydney Morning Herald, September 14, 2014. https://www.shanit.com/docs/SteveJobs_low_tech_parent.pdf.

## 2. The Brain and How It Works

1. Brain Matters. (2020, January 28). *Brain Matters documentary | Early Childhood Development* [Video]. YouTube. https://www.youtube.com/watch?v=Rw_aVnlp0JY.
2. Sentis. (2012, November 6). *Neuroplasticity* [Video]. YouTube. https://www.youtube.com/watch?v=ELpfYCZa87g.

## 3. Knowing What Makes Your Child Tick: Hardwired to Be You

1. PersonalityInsights. (2008, June 18). *Our Personalities Affect Everything We Do - Robert Rohm, Ph.D (DISC expert)* [Video]. YouTube. https://www.youtube.com/watch?v=jky-b8Xh-Xh0.
2. "What is DiSC? Deepen your understanding of yourself and others." Disc Profile. https://www.discprofile.com/what-is-disc.
3. Live On Purpose TV. (2018, January 9). *Teaching Kids Responsibility - Positive Parenting* [Video]. YouTube. https://www.youtube.com/watch?v=1SFIc2LsHyA.
4. Keizer, Kenly. "The Pros and Cons of Screen Time for Kids with ASD." Autism Parenting Magazine, August 5, 2021. https://www.autismparentingmagazine.com/screen-time-kids-with-asd/.
5. "How and why you should limit screen time for kids." Children's Health. https://www.childrens.com/health-wellness/screen-time-guidelines.
6. Howard, Ryan. "How Much Screen Time Is Right For Kids?" Smart Parent Advice, November 18, 2021. https://smartparentadvice.com/screen-time-for-kids/.

## 4. What's All the Fuss About Anyway?

1. "How the Sugar Industry Shifted Blame to Fat." New York Times, September 13, 2016. https://www.nytimes.com/2016/09/13/well/eat/how-the-sugar-industry-shifted-blame-to-fat.html.

2. Dunckley, Victoria L. M.D. "Gray Matters: Too Much Screen Time Damages the Brain." Psychology Today, February 14, 2014. https://www.psychologytoday.com/us/blog/mental-wealth/201402/gray-matters-too-much-screen-time-damages-the-brain.

3. "More Screen Time For Teens Linked To ADHD Symptoms." NPR, heard on Morning Edition, July 17, 2018. https://www.npr.org/sections/health-shots/2018/07/17/629517464/more-screen-time-for-teens-may-fuel-adhd-symptoms.

4. Jean M. Twenge, PhD. *iGen: Why Today's Super-Connected Kids Are Growing Up Less Rebellious, More Tolerant, Less Happy—and Completely Unprepared for Adulthood—and What That Means for the Rest of Us.* Atria Books, 2017.

5. Halina, Victoria. "The Psychology of Social Media — Why We Feel the Need to Share." Victoria Halina, January 30, 2019. https://victoriahalina.medium.com/the-psychology-of-social-media-why-we-feel-the-need-to-share-18c7d2d1236.

6. Makris, Nicole. "For Kids, Bullying by Peers Is Worse Than Abuse from Adults." Healthline, August 1, 2019. https://www.healthline.com/health-news/for-kids-bullying-by-peers-is-worse-than-abuse-from-adults-042815.

## 5. Finding the Power Within You

1. Elizabeth Densley. *The Future is Mine to Design: Finding the Power to Create a Life of Success, Satisfaction and Joy, by Being Open to New Possibilities.* 2018.

2. Mel Robbins. The 5 Second Rule: Transform your Life, Work, and Confidence with Everyday Courage. Savio Republic, 2017.

3. The Arbinger Institute. Leadership and Self-Deception: Getting Out of the Box. Berrett-Koehler Publishers, 2015.
4. Altman, Louise. "Is Self-Deception Keeping You in the Box?" Intentional Communication Consultants, June 2010. https://www.intentionalcommunication.com/is-self-deception-keeping-you-in-the-box/.
5. James J. Crist, Ph.D. What's the Big Deal About Addictions?: Answers and Help for Teens. Free Spirit Publishing, 2021.
6. Elizabeth Densley. The Future is Mine to Design: Finding the Power to Create a Life of Success, Satisfaction and Joy, by Being Open to New Possibilities. 2018.
7. Mary Stevenson. "Footprints in the Sand," Poem For Today, https://poem4today.com/footprints-poem.html.

## 6. You Go First

1. Elizabeth Densley. *The Future is Mine to Design: Finding the Power to Create a Life of Success, Satisfaction and Joy, by Being Open to New Possibilities.* 2018.
2. Duncan, Kirk. 3KeyElements Conference. https://3keyelements.com/.
3. Dana Claudat. (2017, November 1). *Dr. Emoto's Awesome Rice Experiment + Your Superpowerful Intention!* [Video]. YouTube. https://www.youtube.com/watch?v=uDPH18o4dbE.
4. Life-Health-Relax. (2020, March 30). *Masaru Emoto Water Experiment. Music for Stress Relief •40* [Video]. YouTube. https://www.youtube.com/watch?v=z3ykc-dy5H4.
5. TEDx Talks. (2019, August 21). *Look Up! Reduce Your Screen Time and Reclaim Your Life | Melissa Newman | TEDxPLNU* [Video]. YouTube. https://www.youtube.com/watch?v=vf3i9-nSUo8.

# 7. Parenting, Rewards, and Consequences

1. Nicholeen Peck. Welcome to the Calm Parenting Toolkit! [Video]. Teaching Self Government. https://teachingselfgovernment.com/courses/calm-parenting-toolkit/.
2. Nicholeen Peck - Teaching Self Government. (2020, July 28). *How Do Effective Parents Discipline Their Children?* [Video]. YouTube. https://www.youtube.com/watch?v=kCLF0Z1PAmc.
3. Live On Purpose TV. 2020, February 25. *Crucial Skills Parents Need To Master* [Video]. YouTube. https://www.youtube.com/watch?v=2vPa9Ilu7-w.
4. Foster Cline, Jim Fay. Parenting with Love and Logic: Teaching Children Responsibility. NavPress, 2020.
5. Nicholeen Peck - Teaching Self Government. (2020, July 28). How Do Effective Parents Discipline Their Children? [Video]. YouTube. https://www.youtube.com/watch?v=kCLF0Z1PAmc.
6. Live On Purpose TV. 2020, February 25. Crucial Skills Parents Need To Master [Video]. YouTube. https://www.youtube.com/watch?v=2vPa9Ilu7-w.
7. Nicholeen Peck. Welcome to the Calm Parenting Toolkit! [Video]. Teaching Self Government. https://teachingselfgovernment.com/courses/calm-parenting-toolkit/.
8. Live On Purpose TV. 2020, February 25. *Crucial Skills Parents Need To Master* [Video]. YouTube. https://www.youtube.com/watch?v=2vPa9Ilu7-w.
9. Live On Purpose TV. (2020, June 22). *How To Come Up With GOOD CONSEQUENCES* [Video]. YouTube. https://www.youtube.com/watch?v=C6E_1fv9BIs.
10. Nicholeen Peck - Teaching Self Government. (2020, December 4). Setting Consequences For Teenager | Parenting Tips [Video]. YouTube. https://www.youtube.com/watch?v=WYszYjGRMhA.
11. Live On Purpose TV. (2018, August 23). Why Are Consequences An Important Part Of Positive Parenting [Video].

YouTube. https://www.youtube.com/watch?v=-VILGuz5DiU.

12. Live On Purpose TV. (2020, June 22). *How To Come Up With GOOD CONSEQUENCES* [Video]. YouTube. https://www.youtube.com/watch?v=C6E_1fv9BIs.

13. Live On Purpose TV. (2018, August 23). Why Are Consequences An Important Part Of Positive Parenting [Video]. YouTube. https://www.youtube.com/watch?v=-VILGuz5DiU.

## 8. Every Roadblock Has a Detour

1. Elizabeth Densley, DJ Densley. Beyond Reality: The Lost. 2020.

## 9. Finding Your Way Through The Roadblocks Inside You

1. TEDx Talks. (2015, December 16). *Why you don't get what you want; it's not what you expect | Jennice Vilhauer | TEDxPeachtree* [Video]. YouTube. https://www.youtube.com/watch?v=FwLeiY5f7sI.

## 13. Words Are Lethal Weapons: Cyberbullying

1. Sameer Hinduja, Justin W. Patchin. *Bullying Beyond the Schoolyard: Preventing and Responding to Cyberbullying* (2nd edition). Cyberbullying Research Center, 2014.

2. "Cyberbullying Facts: Summarizing What is Currently Known." Cyberbullying Research Center, accessed August 2021. https://cyberbullying.org/facts.

3. Ibid.

4. keithdeltano. (2020, January 22). *Cyberbullying Video for Schools (Lessons / Education) for Middle School and High*

*School Students* [Video]. YouTube. https://www.youtube.-com/watch?v=bW__Dg4588E.

5. "8 Cyberbullying Apps Parents Should Know About." Securly, October 14, 2019. https://blog.securly.-com/2019/10/14/8-anonymous-cyberbullying-apps-you-should-know-about/.

6. "The Annual Bullying Survey 2017." Ditch the Label, 2017 .https://www.ditchthelabel.org/wp-content/up-loads/2017/07/The-Annual-Bullying-Survey-2017-1.pdf

7. "Explainer: What is Snapchat?" Webwise, February 20, 2018 https://www.webwise.ie/parents/explainer-what-is-snapchat-2/.

8. Luke Culhane. (2016, February 8). *Cyber Bullying: Create No Hate* [Video]. YouTube.https://www.youtube.com/watch?v=MV5v0m6pEMs.

9. "7 Tips On Keeping Your Child Safe Online." Securly, July 10, 2018. https://blog.securly.com/2018/07/10/7-tips-on-keeping-your-child-safe-online/.

10. "11 Facts about Cyberbullying." DoSomething.org, accessed August 2021. https://www.dosomething.org/us/facts/11-facts-about-cyber-bullying.

## 14. The Power Within Your Home

1. "Teach Digital Citizenship Skills to Prevent Cyberbullying." StopBullying.gov, accessed August 2021. https://www.stop-bullying.gov/resources/research-resources/digital-citizenship-skills.

2. TEDx Talks. (2014, October 23). *Rethink before you type | Trisha Prabhu | TEDxTeen* [Video]. YouTube. https://www.y-outube.com/watch?v=YkzwHuf6C2U.

3. mrhackio.(2020, August 17). ReThink app quick overview [Video]. YouTube. https://www.youtube.com/watch?v=ozkX-qOQb958.

4. "Children who are being bullied often don't tell their parents." Win Win Parenting, accessed August 2021.

https://www.winwinparenting.com/blog/children-who-are-being-bullied-often-dont-tell-their-parents.

5. "Why Don't Kids Tell Their Parents They're Being Bullied?" What Do I Know? November 4, 2011. https://whatdoino-steve.blogspot.com/2011/11/why-dont-kids-tell-their-parents-theyre.html.

6. "Online Safety and Cyberbullying Resources." Aft - A Union of Professionals, accessed August 2021. https://www.aft.org/online-safety-and-cyberbullying-resources.

7. Google Pay. (2021, March 21). How do I manage privacy controls in Google Pay? [Video] YouTube. https://www.youtube.com/watch?v=8pv9T98T1Oo.

8. Howfinity. (2019, December 7). How To Set Up YouTube Parental Controls [Video]. YouTube. https://www.youtube.com/watch?v=BIB3avfTo4I.

9. Howfinity. (2020, December 12). How to Set Up Parental Controls on iPhone or iPad [Video]. YouTube. https://www.youtube.com/watch?v=pDwOeoc6LAw.

# 15. You're Not Alone

1. Patchin, Justin W. "What Should Your School's Bullying Policy Look Like?" Cyberbullying Research Center, January 31, 2020. https://cyberbullying.org/school-bullying-policy.

2. Cyberbullying Research Center. https://cyberbullying.org/.

# 16. The Ultimate Cyberbully: The Predator

1. TheNightOwl. (2016, September 5). *OBLIVIOUS: An Online Predator PSA* [Video]. Youtube. https://www.youtube.com/watch?v=euc-WcN5IkY.

2. "Sexting." KidsHelpLine. https://kidshelpline.com.au/teens/issues/sexting.

3. "Suitable for 12-18 years - Sexting: talking with teenagers." RaisingChildren.net.au. https://raisingchil-

dren.net.au/teens/entertainment-technology/pornography-sexting/sexting-teens.

4.  TheNightOwl. (2016, September 5). *OBLIVIOUS: An Online Predator PSA* [Video]. Youtube. https://www.youtube.com/watch?v=euc-WcN5IkY.

5.  "Online Predators - Statistics." Puresight. https://www.puresight.com/case_studies/online-predators-statistics/.

6.  Webster, Emma Sarran. "What Is Sexual Grooming? 7 Things to Know About This Abuse Tactic." Allure, July 19, 2017. https://www.allure.com/story/what-is-sexual-grooming-abuse.

7.  Elgersma, Christine. "The Facts About Online Predators Every Parent Should Know." Common Sense Media, July 25, 2017. https://www.commonsensemedia.org/blog/the-facts-about-online-predators-every-parent-should-know.

8.  Webster, Emma Sarran. "What Is Sexual Grooming? 7 Things to Know About This Abuse Tactic." Allure, July 19, 2017. https://www.allure.com/story/what-is-sexual-grooming-abuse.

# ALSO BY ELIZABETH DENSLEY

*The Future is Mine to Design: Finding the Power to Create a Life of Success, Satisfaction and Joy, by Being Open to New Possibilities*

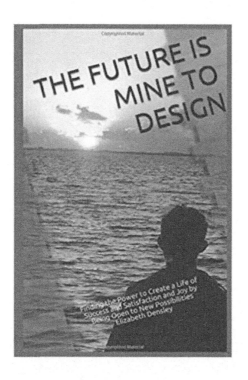

*The Future is Mine to Design* is available separately or as a part of a bundle. This book takes you through the foundational pillars that support Maslow's Hierarchy of Needs in greater detail. The foundational skills that you've learned in *Balancing Your Screen Time as a Family* are further described in detail. No matter the challenge you face, these tools and information can help see you through them.

*Beyond Reality: The Lost*

For our children, we have a middle-grade work of YA fiction about a thirteen-year-old boy named Dex who gets pulled into a video game to help his favorite hero save his people. It includes a free online program that includes comprehension and vocabulary, but most of all, fun activities and treats that tie into each chapter or chapter group.

It's a great way to open conversation and discover what your child is thinking. The first five chapters of this program are free. Just add your purchase order number where indicated and the entire program is yours to explore.

Made in United States
North Haven, CT
28 September 2022

24651984R00189